Food, Stamps, and Income Maintenance

Institute for Research on Poverty
Poverty Policy Analysis Series

Food, Stamps, and Income Maintenance

MAURICE MACDONALD
Institute for Research on Poverty
University of Wisconsin—Madison

ACADEMIC PRESS New York San Francisco London
A Subsidiary of Harcourt Brace Jovanovich, Publishers

ACADEMIC PRESS, INC.
111 Fifth Avenue, New York, New York 10003

United Kingdom Edition published by
ACADEMIC PRESS, INC. (LONDON) LTD.
24/28 Oval Road, London NW1

LIBRARY OF CONGRESS CATALOG CARD NUMBER: 77–77238

ISBN 0–12–464050–8 (cloth)
ISBN 0–12–464052–4 (paper)

PRINTED IN THE UNITED STATES OF AMERICA

Contents

The Institute for Research on Poverty is a national center for research established at the University of Wisconsin in 1966 by a grant from the Office of Economic Opportunity. Its primary objective is to foster basic, multidisciplinary research into the nature and causes of poverty and means to combat it.

In addition to increasing the basic knowledge from which policies aimed at the elimination of poverty can be shaped, the Institute strives to carry analysis beyond the formulation and testing of fundamental generalizations to the development and assessment of relevant policy alternatives.

The Institute endeavors to bring together scholars of the highest caliber whose primary research efforts are focused on the problem of poverty, the distribution of income, and the analysis and evaluation of social policy, offering staff members wide opportunity for interchange of ideas, maximum freedom for research into basic questions about poverty and social policy, and dissemination of their findings.

Foreword

About a decade ago, we discovered another America, where hunger persisted despite unprecedented national economic success. This discovery focused public attention on local food assistance programs supported by the Department of Agriculture, and added to the political impetus of the early war on poverty.

Soon after President Kennedy took office, his Administration initiated several food stamp pilot projects. In the same year that Lyndon Johnson declared his War on Poverty, the Congress enacted the Food Stamp Act of 1964. But in 1967 when the Senate Subcommittee on Employment, Manpower, and Poverty conducted hearings on hunger in Mississippi, and in 1968 when CBS produced its documentary "Hunger in America," the Food Stamp program was still timid in size. In fact, as late as 1972, when Congress made food stamp benefits uniform throughout the country, the program still had only 10 million beneficiaries and paid out only $1.5 billion in benefits. Then in 1973 Congress mandated the provision of food stamp benefits in every jurisdiction in the United States. This change, coupled with the 1974–1975 recession, led to an explosion in food stamp beneficiaries and benefits—to 18 million and $6 billion, respectively, in 1977. From a very small beginning therefore, the Food Stamp program has grown to be an important part of our overall income-maintenance system. A thoroughgoing analysis of the program—its objectives, its achievements, and its shortcomings—is long overdue. Such an analysis is provided by Maurice MacDonald in *Food, Stamps, and Income Maintenance.*

As the title indicates, the author develops a broad perspective on food assistance within the context of the entire income-maintenance system. Besides highlighting the connections among food stamps and other antipoverty programs, he asks whether reducing hunger and malnutrition is better achieved with the Food Stamp program than it would be with a program that simply made cash payments. He also documents some consequences of providing food stamps rather than cash which, given program aims, can be construed as counterproductive.

The monograph covers the history of food assistance and the current program, the impact of administrative structure on recipients' participation and program operation, the income supplementation effect, nutritional effectiveness of food stamps and experimental cash transfers, and the role of the program in the larger income-maintenance system.

MacDonald concludes that although food stamps primarily provide unrestricted income supplementation, from current evidence, they do not have a substantial impact on family nutritional intake. The program does, however, fill gaps in the current welfare system. Thus, whether or not food stamps are preferable to cash assistance, they do augment resources available to needy households, thereby reducing poverty. In addition, MacDonald compares proposals for reform with the current program and offers two alternatives—providing stamps free of charge or replacing them with cash.

This book is the third in the Institute's Poverty Policy Analysis Series. Like its two predecessors—*Progress Against Poverty: A Review of the 1964–1974 Decade* by Robert D. Plotnick and Felicity Skidmore, and *A Decade of Federal Antipoverty Programs: Achievements, Failures, and Lessons* edited by Robert H. Haveman—the book helps us to understand the nature and effects of public programs designed to aid the poor.

Irwin Garfinkel
Director, Institute for
Research on Poverty

Preface

Since 1970 annual federal outlays for the Department of Agriculture's Food Stamp program have increased tenfold—from $600 million to the nearly $6 billion currently received by over 18 million recipients. Because eligibility for these benefits is conditioned only on household income and assets, the program supplements the low wages of the working poor as well as the public assistance payments received by the welfare population. Food producers and distributors also benefit, because aid from the program takes the form of vouchers that may be spent only for food. It is this restriction that identifies food stamps as an in-kind rather than a cash transfer program.

Until recently, policy analysts and laypersons alike have focused primarily on the delivery and impact of cash transfers. Interest in redistributing income in kind has been provoked by the rapid growth of federal food, housing, and medical assistance programs, in conjunction with reticence toward reopening the debate over guaranteed annual incomes.

This monograph evaluates effects of the Food Stamp program on recipient well-being and related benefits for taxpayers and the food industry. It is intended to promote informed decisions about the program's future in the federal income-maintenance system, while offering some general insights for government food aid policy. The study also advances our practical understanding of the relative merits of providing cash versus in-kind transfers.

I am grateful to Robert H. Haveman for suggesting food stamps as a ripe topic for policy analysis and as a vehicle for learning how public assistance programs function. To an even greater extent I owe thanks to Irwin Garfinkel for his continual advice and encouragement. At an important juncture, Jay C. Lipner and E. Lamont Gregory convinced me that my work might actually contribute to the well-being of the poor, greatly enlivening my interest. John Coder, Robert Greenstein, William Hoagland, Wendell Primus, Charles Seagrave, and others I have undoubtedly forgotten helped me learn most of the factual material about food stamps, listened generously to my views, and offered many suggestions. Helpful critiques of earlier drafts were provided by W. Keith Bryant of Cornell University, Stanley H. Masters of the University of Wisconsin, and Janice Peskin of the Office of Income Security Policy, DHEW. Katharine Mochon edited my writing. Daniel Dodds and Robert T. McGee assisted me in research. I profusely thank Wanda Montgomery, Mary Ellen Rodriguez, Julie Roh, and the rest of the Institute typists who patiently processed the numerous versions of each chapter. Person-in-the-street views were freely and persuasively provided by Jeanne MacDonald. Finally, my faculty colleagues and students in the Consumer Science Program of the University's School of Family Resources deserve praise for unselfishly facilitating my research.

None of these fine people are responsible for any mistakes and confusions that remain.

An Analytical History of the Food Stamp Program

According to Richard P. Nathan, formerly Deputy Under-Secretary of HEW for Welfare Reform, the expansion of the Food Stamp program since 1964 is the "most important change in public welfare policy in the United States since the passage of the Social Security Act in 1935 [1975, p. 9]," — food stamps have filled gaps in welfare programs that have grown out of the 1935 act, making the overall mix of programs more equitable and adequate. Understanding how food stamps became a major feature of the "welfare state" requires an historical perspective on federal food assistance policy. In the light of this perspective, the effect of changes in program design on food stamp enrollment can be assessed. Such an assessment will necessarily be quantitative in nature, and will thus suggest the extent of future program growth.

FOOD ASSISTANCE PRIOR TO 1945

The basic legislation first authorizing food assistance for low-income persons in the United States was initiated during the Great Depression, in the form of Section 32 of Public Law 72-320 (The Potato Control Act of 1935). This section provided 30% of the receipts from U.S. Customs could be used by the secretary of agriculture to encourage exports of agricultural products, to finance adjustments in agricultural production, and to "encourage the domestic consumption of such commodities or products by diverting them, by payment of benefits or indemnities or by other means, from the natural channels of trade and commerce." This last authorization permitted the purchase of surplus farm products for distribution to needy families and school church programs, administered through the Federal Surplus Commodities Corporation (FSCC). The primary aim of the FSCC, however was not to meet the food needs of relief recipients, but, rather, to support farm prices. Because the FSCC was controlled by the Department of Agriculture's Agricultural Adjustment Administration, the emphasis on strengthening agricultural markets is hardly surprising.

Dissatisfaction with the surplus commodities program on the part of recipients and food retailers contributed to the initiation of the first food stamp program, which operated from 1939 to 1943. Advocates for needy households complained that direct distribution was unsatisfactory because foods (including perishables) were distributed monthly. This caused difficulties for recipients in budgeting food consumption: Much higher consumption (mostly of perishables) occurred immediately after distribution than later in the month. Moreover, because the kinds of foods received depended on whatever happened to be in surplus, nutritional needs of recipients were largely ignored. These facts provided potent argument for change, as the severity of the depression generated widespread public concern about nutritional deficiencies and starvation. Food retailers joined the call for reform in food assistance because they disliked having their normal trade channels bypassed by the FSCC. Eventually, lobbying efforts on behalf of the food industry led to agreement on a food stamp plan that began in May 1939 with funding authorized by Section 32.

The purpose of the first food stamp program was to increase domestic food consumption through regular business channels. This goal was to be accomplished by providing two kinds of stamps to welfare recipients. The stamps could be used to buy food from authorized retailers. Participants were to purchase a minimum number of orange stamps at face value. Upon purchasing the orange stamps, the recipient was provided free blue stamps (usually on a 2:1 orange to blue stamp ratio). These blue stamps represented a federal subsidy that could be used only to purchase foods appearing on a monthly list of surplus commodities designated by the secretary of agriculture. The orange stamps were issued in amounts supposedly equal to the recipient family's normal food expenditures and could be spent on any food item. By ensuring that orange stamps were issued only in amounts equal to normal food expenditure (never less), it was thought that income normally spent on food would not be diverted to nonfood items owing to the subsidy embodied in the free blue stamps.

In his outstanding study of the two-stamp program, Joseph D. Coppock (1947) found it to be less than fully effective as a method for strengthening the agricultural economy. Coppock compared the increase in expenditures on all foods attributable to participation in the program to that expected from a direct cash subsidy. He concluded that although eligibles would have spent 45% of any cash income increment on food, 60% of the food subsidy actually went for food. Hence, the first food voucher program was not much more effective as a stimulant to the farm economy than cash subsidies would have been. It appears that participants did not buy more food than they would have if the blue stamps were not issued; they simply did not use all their orange stamps. That is, normally purchased surplus foods were purchased with blue stamps. No steps were taken to curtail this practice because the need for the program as a method to control the farm surplus gradually disappeared as World War II progressed. It would seem, from Coppock's analysis, that the World War II stamp program was probably as advantageous to food retailers as it was for food producers. From the recipients' standpoint, the program provided gains not offered under the FSCC. "The food trade added their services to the surplus food distributed under the Food Stamp Plan and reaped their margins in return [Bryant, 1973]."

The two-stamp scheme did tend to restrict the recipients' ability to substitute nonfood for food items, and it did allow more choice of food types than under the commodity program. In addition, recipients received the services of retailers, including storage and conveniences not available under the FSCC plan. Finally, Bryant (1973) suggests that the social stigma associated with standing in line to receive FSCC commodities may have been greater than that attached to using food stamps in retail stores. On the whole, then, all concerned parties benefited from the two-stamp programs.

During its operation, the first stamp program served approximately 4 million persons annually, at a total cost of $261 million. As the number of unemployed fell and the farm surplus disappeared due to wartime conditions, both the FSCC and food stamp plan withered. In March 1943, food

TABLE 1.1
Participation in and Federal Costs of the
Commodity Distribution Program, Selected
Years through 1970 (Peak Values)

Fiscal year	Number of persons (in thousands)	Federal government costs[a] (in thousands of dollars)
1936	10,114	31,792
1938	8,801	35,375
1939	12,690	66,264
1943	2,426	12,589
1945	360	1,800
1946	58	75
1950	248	6,038
1951	1,225	6,812
1953	114	360
1955	3,291	61,948
1957	3,485	77,918
1961	6,384	139,988
1963	7,019	204,391
1964	6,135	197,144
1966	4,781	134,060
1968	3,491	124,016
1970	4,129	289,423

Source: USDA, Food and Nutrition Service (1974).
[a] Federal costs of purchasing, processing, packaging, and transporting surplus commodities to receiving points chosen by the state agency.

stamps were terminated, and expenditures for the FSCC reached their low point of $180 million in 1945 (see Table 1.1).

Later, when public concern for the nutritional status of the poor would again coincide with a period of large farm surpluses, the experience of the first food stamp program and the FSCC would provide firm ground from which to judge the relative merits of two different approaches to food assistance—food stamps and direct commodity distribution. Thus, although the first food stamp program was not large even by the standards of public welfare expenditures during the 1940s, its impact on subsequent food assistance policy may have been substantial.

POSTWAR FOOD PROGRAMS

During the postwar period, the rapid accumulation of farm surpluses, combined with concern for the needy abroad led Congress to authorize the use of surplus commodities for free distribution to needy foreign countries. Two laws authorized these activities, Section 416 of the Agricultural Act of 1949, and Public Law 83-480 (the Agricultural Trade Development and Assistance Act of 1954). To some extent, the disposal of surplus abroad under the authorization of Section 416 limited the amount of free food distributed domestically via the food distribution program. Therefore, in the 1950s, Congress attempted to put more emphasis on the domestic need for food surplus than that which existed in the early postwar period. Still, as shown in Table 1.1, there were sizable numbers of domestic commodity recipients throughout the 1950s. In fact the domestic food distribution program grew until the mid-1960s, and then declined as the era of large farm surpluses ended. Without examining the specifics of the postwar food distribution program, it appears that the level of program activity was largely determined by the availability of surplus foods. Today, direct distribution of commodities via the food distribution program is limited primarily to Indian reservations. The Food Stamp program now handles the bulk of the food assistance responsibilities of the Department of Agriculture.

ORIGINS OF THE CURRENT FOOD STAMP PROGRAM

During the decade following the demise of the first food stamp program, Vermont's Senator George Aiken introduced seven separate bills proposing a revised food stamp program with striking similarities to the program we now have. Under Aiken's proposals, needy families would have spent no more than 40% of their income on stamps sufficient to buy a nutritionally adequate diet, and low-income recipients would pay less for the stamps than high-income recipients. Aiken's efforts to resurrect the program were supported by Congresswoman Leonor Sullivan of Missouri, who introduced her first bill to enact a food stamp program in 1954. The persistent efforts of Representative Sullivan, in conjunction with public pressure to make productive use of the renewed accumulation of food surpluses following the Korean War, led to the enactment of Section 201 of Public Law 84-540 (the Agricultural Act of 1956), which directed the secretary of agriculture to prepare an analysis of food stamp plans.

The analysis by the Department of Agriculture was unfavorable on two accounts. First, it was demonstrated that in order to expand food consumption substantially, families with both modest and low incomes would have to be allowed to participate, and appropriations would have to be large. Second, for the purposes of disposing of seasonal or localized surpluses, food stamps were deemed less effective than existing Food Distribution efforts.

Although the analysis neglected to consider the proposed program's nutritional benefits, these benefits were perceived to be important by many, because 1957 and 1958 brought continued pressure for a food stamp program. Eventually, in the 1958 extension of Public Law 480, efforts by Congresswoman Sullivan, Senator Hubert Humphrey, and others brought about authorization for a 2-year pilot food stamp program, funded at an annual level of $250 million. Nevertheless, consistent with its longstanding position that the primary goal of food assistance was to create markets for surplus products, the Eisenhower administration chose not to experiment with food stamps. Although the Republican executive branch recognized the need for some form of income assistance for needy families, it did not favor expanding the welfare responsibilities of the federal government, viewing such responsibilities as a charge for state and local governments. But with the 1960 election of a Democratic president, the executive branch began to embrace a different philosophy about the role of federal food programs.

While campaigning for the West Virginia primary, John F. Kennedy is said to have had "a depressing close-up view of the surplus commodity program [Schlossberg 1975, p. 12]." Perhaps as a result of this experience, President Kennedy's first executive order in 1961 instituted eight pilot food stamp projects, located in West Virginia and six other states. These eight pilot programs were later expanded to 43, and by March 1964, 392,400 persons were participating at a federal cost of $29 million. On average, for a mother and three children, the program provided $64 in stamps per month, for which the family paid $34 of its monthly income of $70 (Schlossberg 1975, p. 12).

Except for the use of a single stamp, the pilot food stamp program was quite similar to the program of 1939–1943. Certified families, mostly from the public welfare rolls, exchanged "normal food expenditures" for food coupons of greater monetary value. Only certain imported foods could not be purchased at participating retail outlets.

Preliminary evaluations of the first eight pilot projects were favorable. However, because perishable food items, not considered surplus, com-

prised a substantial portion of the recipients' purchases, economists concluded that food stamps could not eliminate the farm surpluses of the
mid-1950s and early 1960s (Hoagland, 1976). Yet, as a program for
which income was the sole condition of eligibility, the stamps were reaching needy people who did not fall into categories eligible for other forms of
public assistance. Undoubtedly, this fact offset the negative findings with
respect to the farm surplus. Moreover, studies of the diets of families in two
pilot projects revealed that from 33% to almost 50% of the families had
diets that supplied the family with 100% or more of the allowances for
eight nutrients recommended by the National Research Council. But
among comparable nonparticipating families, only 28% had good diets
(Steiner, 1971). Furthermore, food sales had increased by 8% in a sample
of pilot retailers. Based on these findings, 31 new pilot projects were
opened, almost exclusively in the districts of Democratic congressional
representatives.

The pilot program was gradually expanded under the administrative
powers granted Secretary of Agriculture Orville Freeman by Section 32 of
the Agriculture Adjustment Act. During this expansion the Kennedy administration became convinced that the stamp program represented, in
Freeman's words, "a better and more efficient means than commodity
distribution for channeling more of the abundance of American agriculture
to families in economic need [U.S. Senate, 1964]." Nevertheless, when a
bill to authorize a nationwide program was introduced in Congress, Southern Democrats and Republicans (especially farm bloc members), were
reluctant to endorse a public assistance effort in the guise of an agricultural
program. This obstacle was overcome by a logrolling arrangement between backers of wheat and cotton price supports and proponents of food
stamps (Steiner, 1971). The result was the Food Stamp Act of 1964.

The Food Stamp Act

The 1964 act initially authorized a 3-year program,

> in order to promote the general welfare, that the nation's abundance of food
> should be utilized cooperatively by the State, the Federal Government, and
> local government units to the maximum extent practicable to safeguard the
> health and raise the levels of nutrition among low-income households [P.L.
> 8-525, 78 Stat.].

To restate, the Food Stamp Act was to be implemented with cooperation
at all levels of government to achieve two goals: (a) utilization of the

nd (*b*) promotion of the nutritional well-being of low-
Although the dual goals of this act seemed compatible,
gress who were aware of the findings from pilot project
imably understood that the ability of the stamp program
s food was limited relative to its potential impact on the
purchasing power of low-income households. Moreover, since the act
granted the option of establishing food stamp projects to state agencies
authorized to administer local public assistance programs, members of
congress from conservative areas could vote for passage, secure in the
knowledge that their constituents could still decide not to offer the program. (The act prohibited operation of both a Food Stamp and a Food
Distribution program in the same locality.)

Purchase requirements—the cash amount purchasers had to pay for
their stamp allotment—were specified on the federal level by the U.S.
Department of Agriculture (USDA). But, reflecting the basic orientation of
the act toward state jurisdiction, eligibility standards for monthly allowable
income cut-off levels were set by the states, along with resource or assets
tests, usually consistent with the state's criteria for public assistance eligibility. This latitude initially fostered considerable interstate variation in implementation of the act. One difference of particular interest to food assistance advocates was that some states had relatively more stamp recipients
than others, even after crude adjustments for variations in the size of the
target populations. In 1969, a Senate committee concluded that

> Nationally only 21.6 percent of the poor people living in counties with food
> stamp programs participate in the program. Only in the State of Washington
> and the District of Columbia do food stamp programs reach over 40 percent of
> the poor. Seven states have programs that reach less than 15 percent of their
> poor. Only 116, or 10 percent of all countries with food stamp programs reach
> 40 percent or more of their poor [U.S. Senate, 1969].

A related cause for concern was that among all counties switching from
commodities to food stamps during 1961–1968, there was an average
decline of 40% in the number of participants (Steiner, 1971). As a result of
these concerns the state and federal regulations established pursuant to the
Food Stamp Act of 1964 became the subject of considerable scrutiny,
focusing on factors that might restrict program participation levels.

Inquiries

Two inquiries into the operation of the food stamp program deserve
special mention in regard to the participation issue. In 1967, the Senate

Subcommittee on Employment, Manpower, and Poverty took responsibility for congressional oversight of food stamps. Committee members, including Senators Joseph Clark and Robert F. Kennedy, traveled to the Mississippi Delta to investigate reports of difficulties in the transition from the commodities program to food stamps. As a result of the report from the committee members with first-hand knowledge of the situations, the full committee petitioned President Johnson to take steps that would increase the size of the food stamp recipient population wherever conditions of acute hunger and malnutrition might exist. Their recommendations included free stamps for people without cash incomes, lower purchase requirements in general, and investigations of alleged overcharges for stamps. In addition, the senators urged that free surplus commodities be distributed through local private, as well as public, agencies. The president responded by delegating authority to the fledgling Office of Economic Opportunity, which provisionally accepted a claim by the USDA that USDA could not legally authorize the desired actions under the Food Stamp Act. Nevertheless, bowing to continuing pressure from what came to be called the "hunger lobby," USDA reduced purchase requirements in Mississippi to 50 cents per person per month late in 1967, and began to negotiate with Mississippi officials to guarantee federal funding of households that could not pay even the reduced purchase prices (Steiner, 1971).

Simultaneously, the self-appointed Citizens Board of Inquiry into Hunger and Malnutrition in the United States (1968) was preparing a study entitled *Hunger U.S.A.* This study, released in April 1968, identified 256 "hunger counties"—counties that the Board found to be locales for chronic hunger and malnutrition. Among the remedies this provocative report proposed was a free food stamp program in every locality. Then in May 1968, a CBS television program "Hunger in America," disseminated the findings of the Citizen Board to a wider audience, concluding that the Department of Agriculture had been reluctant to exercise emergency powers.[1] The ensuing controversy over *Hunger U.S.A.* and "Hunger in America" led Ralph Abernathy and the Poor People's Campaign to confront the Department of Agriculture directly. At about the same time, the Senate established a Select Committee on Nutrition and Human Need, chaired by Senator George McGovern. Thus, as the presidential election of 1968 got underway, food program policies were an important political issue.

---

[1] A transcript of "Hunger in America" appeared in the *Congressional Record*, May 29, 1968, p. S6637.

The Nixon Years

However, major program modifications were delayed until President Nixon acted in May 1969. In his hunger message to Congress, Nixon asserted that the moment was ". . . at hand to put an end to hunger in America itself for all time." In addition, the president recommended that food stamps were to have priority over food distribution, that the most needy should receive free food stamps, that there be a ceiling of 30% of income for the purchase price for stamp allotments, and that stamp allotments should be increased. After interim modifications during 1969 by Secretary of Agriculture Hardin, Congress eventually adopted the Nixon proposals in its 1971 amendments to the Food Stamp Act of 1964 (Public Law 91-671, 1971). The 1971 amendments also set uniform national income and resource eligibility standards, and increased the federal share of state administrative costs to 50% (Hoagland, 1976). Table 1.2 summarizes the changes in the program's benefits schedule from 1970 to 1972. On average, recipient benefits doubled during this period (Holmer, 1976). Overall, the 1971 changes increased federal involvement in the program's administration and led to rising program participation. As shown in Table 1.3, program costs and caseloads accelerated rapidly after 1970. In 1973, further amendments mandated that all counties across the country offer food stamps as of July 1974, to complete the switchover from food distribution to food stamps. Thus by conscious congressional design, the food stamp program finally became available to all eligible low-income persons.

In part, the 1973 congressional decision to expand the program can be explained by the earlier failure of Congress to adopt President Nixon's Family Assistance Plan (FAP). Since it is generally agreed that the defeat of this plan was very narrow—an indication of broad support for a guaranteed income—one congressional motive for mandating a nationwide food stamp program could have been a desire to alleviate a generally recognized need for a guaranteed family income. In other words, extending food stamps to all areas can be interpreted as a gradual welfare reform. A brief review of the role food stamps played in the controversy over the Family Assistance Plan helps to amplify this conjecture.

In *Nixon's Good Deed*, Vincent J. and Vee Burke (1974) report that the administration's welfare working group initially decided to eliminate food stamps from their Family Assistance Plan. It was thought that supplementing family assistance with food stamps would be too costly. In a press briefing after announcement of FAP, newsman Nick Kotz asked if this

TABLE 1.2
Food Stamp Purchase Requirements and Monthly Allotments for a Household of Four Members, Selected Months, 1970–1972

Monthly income	December 1970		January 1971		January 1972	
	Purchase requirement	Monthly coupon allotment	Purchase requirement	Monthly coupon allotment	Purchase requirement	Monthly coupon allotment
Under $30	$ 2	$60	$ 2	$106	$ 0	$103
Under $50	20	64	10	106	10	108
Under $100	100	78	25	106	25	108
Under $200	200	92	54	106	54	108
Under $250	250	100	72	106	72	108

Source: USDA, Food and Nutrition Service (1974).

11

TABLE 1.3
Food Stamp Program Overview 1964–1975

Fiscal year	Number of states	Number of program areas	Participants (in thousands)	Federal bonus stamp cost (in millions of dollars)
1964 (pilot phase)	22	43	360	28.6
1965	29	110	632	32.5
1966	41	324	1,218	64.8
1967	42	838	1,831	105.5
1968	44	1027	2,419	173.1
1969	44	1489	3,222	228.8
1970	46	1747	6,457	549.7
1971	47	2027	10,584	1522.7
1972	47	2126	10,594	1797.3
1973	48	2228	12,106	2131.4
1974	50	3062	13,524	2714.1
1975	50	3075	19,238	4404.9

Source: Hoagland (1976, p. 16).

might mean some families would suffer a cut in aid, because most families eligible under Aid to Families with Dependent Children would get no greater cash benefit under FAP and many already received food stamps as well. However, on August 11, 1969, President Nixon's special welfare reform message to Congress reported that needy persons ineligible for FAP (mostly married couples without children and nonaged, able-bodied single persons) would still qualify for food stamps, up to $300 per person per year. Families eligible for FAP were to receive cash payments instead of food stamps, implying the aid reductions Kotz had pointed out. This position was immediately attacked by the hunger lobby, and the Nixon administration backed down.

> Thus, within seven and one-half months after taking office, a Republican president had called for two new federal income-guarantee plans, whereas before the nation had none. If Congress enacted both, the food stamp and FAP cash guarantee program together would assure a minimum income of $2,320 for a family of four (provided it lived in a county that distributed the stamps): $1,600 in cash and $720 in food stamps. (A family with zero income of its own would have to pay 30 percent of its FAP cash benefit, $480, to receive food stamps worth $1,200) [Burke and Burke 1974, p. 122].

QUANTIFYING SOURCES OF PROGRAM GROWTH

Having reviewed the origins of the current Food Stamp Program and its growth from a few pilot projects into the current expanded program, we shall now analyze the sources of program growth in greater detail. Based on available studies, we shall attempt to consolidate and extend our remarks by quantifying the relative importance of three factors that contributed to the expansion of the program during the 1970s. In chronological order, these factors were

1. The liberalization of program benefits during the Nixon Administration in 1970, which considerably reduced stamp prices and increased stamp allotments (see Table 1.2)
2. The extension of the program to all counties after July 1974 under the 1973 congressional amendment
3. The 1974–1976 recession, which, combined with food price inflation, increased the need for food assistance to low-income households

In addition to contributing to a better understanding of the sources of growth in food stamp program rolls, in this section we shall also suggest the extent and likelihood of continued growth of the Food Stamp Program.

Figure 1.1 illustrates quarterly participation data for food stamps and food distribution combined, and separately for food stamps, over the period 1967–1976. The figure also identifies the onset of the 1970 liberalization of program benefits, the 1973 mandate for wider geographic dispersion, and of the starting quarter for the most recent economic recession. The figure clearly demonstrates a rise in the Food Stamp Program caseload subsequent to each of these significant events. However, the most dramatic increase in participant numbers is associated with the 1970 benefit increases, reflecting the doubled value of the average bonus per recipient. Geographic extension and the recession account for the continued growth of the program after 1971. About 1 year prior to the onset of the recession (designated as October 1974, by the National Bureau of Economic Research), food prices began to rocket, eventually increasing at an annual rate of 20.7% between the first and second half of 1973 (Hoagland, 1976). Thereafter, continuing food price inflation combined with increasing unemployment and declining personal incomes increased the need for food stamps on the part of low-income households. These factors explain a sub-

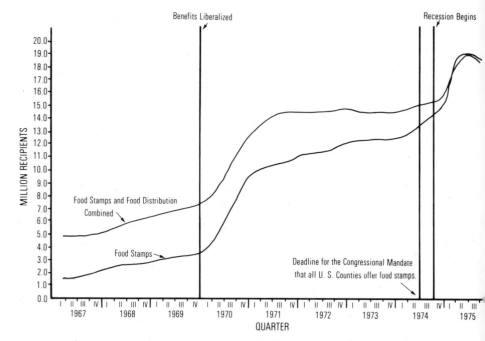

Figure 1.1. *Seasonally adjusted quarterly average numbers of recipients. Food stamps and food stamps and food distribution combined. Note: Administrative modifications doubled average benefits in 1970; recession starting point is from official National Bureau of Economic Research figures. Data supplied by Congressional Budget Office (1976).*

stantial part of the increase from 15 million food stamp participants in the third quarter of 1974 to nearly 19.2 million in the second quarter of 1975 (see Figure 1.1). According to estimates derived by Charles Seagrave (1975) about one-quarter of this increase can be attributed to the rise in unemployment associated with the recession. Of course, part of the total increase was also due to the addition of recipients from areas that had neither food stamps nor food distribution prior to July 1974. In addition, Guam, Puerto Rico, and the Virgin Islands began distributing food stamps to their islanders in 1974. By the end of fiscal 1975, Puerto Rico alone had 1.7 million food stamp recipients, almost triple the number of Puerto Rican food distribution recipients (Seagrave, 1975).

Nevertheless, there can be little doubt that the recession played a large part in the most recent caseload expansion. As documented by William Hoagland (1976) for the Congressional Budget Office, the greatest growth took place in the recipient category known as non-public-assistance recipients, as opposed to public assistance recipients categorically eligible for food stamps and receiving other forms of public assistance, primarily AFDC. According to Hoagland, most of the recipient growth occurred among intact households, where both parents lived together and the father was employed or employable. In support of this claim Figure 1.2 presents the appropriate time series of quarterly participation averages by subcategory.

The availability of a detailed time-series analysis of program growth conducted by Martin Holmer (1976) allows a more careful examination of the relative importance of the three major influences at interest here.[2] Holmer's study led to the following findings:

1. Without the increase in program benefits, but with the expansion of the program attributable to both increased geographical coverage and recession, the 1975 caseload would have been less than half its actual size, and subsidy costs would have been less than one-third their actual value.
2. Assuming the increase in program benefits under Nixon without the 1973 amendment for a nationwide program, followed by the recession, the 1975 program would have been roughly 60% of its actual size for both subsidy costs and recipient numbers.
3. Liberalizing program benefits and extending geographical coverage in the absence of the recession would have resulted in program subsidies and caseloads that were roughly 75% of their cor-

---

[2]Holmer's study improves upon an earlier participation study by Fred K. Hines (1972) by developing a quarterly time-series regression model that effectively explains the 1961–1975 variation in both program caseload and bonus stamp costs. The explanatory variables in the equation predicting bonus costs included a dummy variable indicating the period of pilot programs prior to the 1964 Food Stamp Act; a dummy variable to mark the early 1970 change in the benefit levels and an index that adjusts the National average bonus value for changes in the composition of areas providing food stamps. In the caseload model, Holmer's explanatory variables were the ratio of the average monthly bonus to monthly per capita disposable personal income; the seasonally adjusted aggregate unemployment rate for each quarter; the total public assistance caseload at the start of each quarter; seasonal dummy variables indicating quarters two through four; a variable that measures the surge of caseload openings when new programs began; and a dummy variable to date the 1971 implementation of President Nixon's administrative reforms.

Holmer then performed counterfactual simulations of food stamp growth by holding constant the values of selected explanatory variables while allowing others to take on their actual values. Thus he was able to estimate the caseload size and bonus stamp costs that would have prevailed during 1975 in the absence of each of the three major influences on program growth, taken separately.

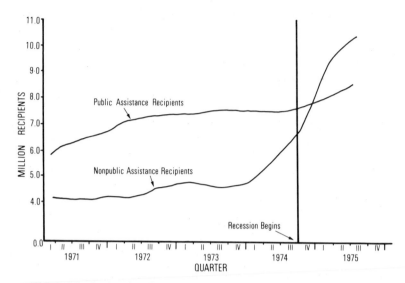

Figure 1.2. *Seasonally adjusted average numbers of food stamp recipients. Public assistance and non-public-assistance categories. Note: Recession starting point is from official National Bureau of Economic Research figures. Data supplied by Congressional Budget Office (1976).*

responding 1975 values. The simulation that produced this finding assumes that the unemployment rate would have remained constant after 1970, and that personal disposable income would have grown at a rate comensurate with this favorable unemployment experience.

In brief, the 1969–1970 increase in program benefits accounts for most of the program's growth since that time, although expanding geographical coverage was nearly as important, and the effects of the recession were not minor. Because further expansion of geographical coverage is not possible, if benefits are maintained at current levels and the economy continues on a course of sustained growth, Holmer expects the program to grow moderately during the next few years, barring an increase in the rate of participation among program eligibles. As of 1976, less than half of all eligibles participated in the program, suggesting the potential for further expansion.

In assessing factors that could contribute to an increased rate of program participation, publicity about the program's growth is often mentioned. In this regard, the potential impact of program regulations regarding publicity about the program deserves further attention.

Outreach

An "outreach" amendment of the 1964 act required state agencies to undertake "effective action, including the uses of services provided by other federally funded agencies and organizations, to inform low-income households concerning the availability and benefits of the food stamp program [*Federal Register*, 1975, p. 1883]." Until 1975, the states did very little to comply with this requirement. Consequently, food assistance advocates filed a series of court actions to force the USDA to implement outreach efforts, beginning in Minnesota with *Bennett* v. *Butz* (1974, 386 F. Supp. 10–59, C. D. Minn.) and followed by suits in 17 other states. In April 1975, USDA complied with the final decision and order of Judge Miles Lord, who presided in *Bennett* v. *Butz,* by issuing a new set of outreach regulations. At the request of attorneys for the Food Research and Action Center, a public interest law firm, the new regulations established one full-time outreach coordinator in each state who reported to the USDA on state outreach activities. These state coordinators are also charged with developing and monitoring annual state outreach plans, including efforts directed toward the special needs of the elderly, disabled, migrants, rural poor, and ethnic groups. In areas where these efforts are conscientiously undertaken, they have probably contributed to modest expansions in local caseloads.

SUMMARY AND OUTLINE

Underlying the development of food stamps from a scheme to augment depression relief and surplus disposal activities into the primarily welfare-oriented program of today are two groups with divergent interests—the needy and the agriculture bloc—reaching a series of compromises that allowed both to partially achieve their major aims. With the passage of the Food Stamp Act in 1964, advocates for the needy extracted a food assistance program from a department that oversees the interests of primarily nonneedy food producers and distributors. In return, the agricultural bloc received a program outwardly tailored for its benefit, in addition to timely support for various farm bills by urban congressional representatives. Food retailers influenced this transition from surplus disposal to nutrition assistance by lobbying for food distribution through regular channels of trade. After 1964, the gradual and then sudden disappearance of the farm surplus helped to advance the idea that the food stamp program should be restructured to put the assistance of recipients as the primary goal. This recognition eventually resulted in a liberalization of program benefits under President Nixon, whose party had long opposed the food stamp program. However, farm bloc Republicans had less to lose when the surplus disappeared. Thus, it appears that changes in the conditions of agricultural markets influenced the terms of trade between the direct and indirect beneficiaries of food assistance, altering the political context in which the two major interests bargained.

Analysis of the three major changes in program regulations since the enactment of the Food Stamp Act of 1964 demonstrates that the most important modification affecting program growth occurred when the Nixon administration effectively doubled the average benefit available to recipient households. Subsequent nationwide expansion of the program also had a substantial impact on costs and caseloads. However, the most recent burst of program activity can be attributed to the recession (perhaps facilitated by outreach), which had its greatest impact on participation among nonpublic-assistance households. Over the next few years, program growth is expected to be modest, unless publicity about the program contributes to a substantial rise in participation among existing eligible households.

With the historical groundwork laid Chapter 2 completes preparation for subsequent analysis with a discussion of administrative structure and the corresponding delegation of responsibility to various levels of government. A fairly detailed consideration of regulations and administrative practices that affect program performance follows and implications for equity in benefit distribution and for administrative efficiency are discussed. In short, Chapter 2 provides a concise introduction to the content and implementation of the rules that govern the food stamp program.

Chapter 3 is the first of three chapters comprising an evaluation of the program's major economic functions, which include income supplementation, augmenting the demand for food, and associated effects on recipients' nutritional status. Relative to cash transfers, food stamps have both advantages and disadvantages in performing each of these functions. Chapter 3 begins with a general discussion of the relative merits of the program and then attempts to quantify the extent to which food stamps induce greater food expenditures than expected from cash transfers of equivalent cost to the taxpayer in an effort to determine how effectively the program supplements incomes vis à vis stimulating demand for food. Recipients gain both general purchasing power and food-restricted purchasing power. The program allows food stamps to be used in place of cash outlays for some foods. Thus, the money that would ordinarily be spent on those foods becomes available for other uses. The major conclusion of Chapter 3 is that food stamps provide essentially unrestricted income supplementation. Different assumptions about the political reasons for the public's decision to offer food stamps produce various policy implications.

Chapter 4 examines the nutritional effectiveness of food stamps and experimental cash transfers. A simple model of the nutritional achievement process is used to clarify how food stamps might influence household nutrient intake. Survey research conducted in California and Pennsylvania for the purpose of comparing the nutritional status of food stamp recipients and nonrecipients is then interpreted. Both studies tentatively conclude that food stamps probably do not have a substantial impact on household nutrient intake. On the other hand, evidence collected in North Carolina for the Rural Negative Income Tax experiments suggests that more generous cash transfers do improve nutritional status, although experimental evidence from Iowa indicates the opposite. However, even assuming the most favorable of the nutritional impacts detected in these studies, crude estimates demonstrate that for nutritional purposes, both the food stamps and the cash transfers are cost ineffective.

Thus the stage is set for Chapter 5, which looks at food stamps as one component of the larger income-maintenance system. After examining the characteristics of food stamp users, the problems and advantages that arise when food stamp users receive benefits from other transfer programs are discussed. Survey data are used to study the importance of multiple benefit combinations for benefit adequacy and work disincentives. In addition, we estimate a substantial contribution of food stamps toward reducing the official poverty count, for the nation and by state. Using this information we find that the Food Stamp Program fills gaps in coverage available under traditional welfare and social insurance programs, resulting in a more equitable and adequate income maintenance system.

However, this is not to say that the program has reached its full potential. In fact, only about one-half of all persons eligible currently participate in the program. Chapter 6 is devoted to documenting and explaining this low rate of participation. Based on information obtained from the Michigan Panel Study of Income Dynamics, it appears that small benefit amounts for some recipients does not account for the widespread reluctance to participate. A multivariate analysis of the characteristics distinguishing Michigan Panel eligible participants from eligible nonparticipants provides evidence to evaluate hypotheses based on a rudimentary model that considers information, stigma, and access costs of participation. For the most part, our analysis is only suggestive with respect to specific policies for increasing program participation, except to say that as benefits rise, so does participation.

Chapter 7 consolidates and extends prior findings by analyzing alternative futures for the program. This final chapter first summarizes and evaluates the most important provisions of three major reform proposals generated by President Ford and the 94th Congress in response to widespread concern about program effectiveness during the 1974–1975 economic recession. In comparison with the current program, it has been estimated that these proposals represent only modest changes in both total program costs and the distribution of benefits among broad classes of recipients. Going beyond those widely endorsed proposals, two alternatives are considered that are likely to expand the program—providing food stamps free of charge, or replacing food stamp benefits with cash. The former has been proposed by Senators Robert Dole and George McGovern, while the latter is often mentioned as a tool for gradual welfare reform. Distinctions between these two alternatives for recipient benefits and corresponding increments in program costs are presented. Finally, the choice among alternatives for the future of the program is in part a value judgment, and is left for the readers to determine.

How the Food Stamp
Program Works

2

Chapter 1 provided an introduction to the administrative structure of the Food Stamp program; this chapter describes how users interact with agency workers in completing the various steps that must be taken for an eligible household to acquire and spend the stamps.[1] As in any federal program, these steps proceed along lines dictated by complicated regulations. Hence we present a detailed discussion of the regulations pertaining to the program's means test, benefit determination, definition of the household recipient unit, and work registration requirement. Next we survey procedures intended to maintain program integrity—quality control, accountability for cash and coupons, and supervision of the food retailers who redeem the stamps. In addition to providing a general guide to the structure of food stamps as a federal transfer program, much of the information contained in this chapter will facilitate understanding of subsequent analytic chapters.

---

[1]For further information about program operations, two sources are especially worthwhile; see Food Research and Action Center (1976) and subsequent biannual versions, and U.S. Congress, House of Representatives (1976).

ADMINISTRATIVE STRUCTURE

The administrative tasks required in operating the food stamp program are shared by federal, state, and local governments. At the federal level, the duties of the USDA Food and Nutrition Service include: instituting program rules and structure; responsibility for producing, handling, distributing, and refunding the food stamps; supervising data collection and quality control procedures; and generally overseeing program activities. State governments are responsible for conducting outreach campaigns to inform eligibles about the program; collecting data on program characteristics; and maintaining federal standards of administrative efficiency. At the local level, county food stamp agencies deal directly with stamp recipients and are responsible for serving them. Thus, the success of the food stamp program is highly dependent on the skill and care of food stamp caseworkers and their supervisors.

According to estimates derived by Kenneth Clarkson (1975) for 1973, the average administrative and operating cost of transferring $1 in bonus stamps was 9 cents, including costs borne by states and localities, as well as by the federal government. For fiscal year 1977, the U.S. House Agriculture Committee Staff (1976) estimated that the federal administrative costs of the program amounted to $400 million, or roughly 7% of total program costs.

Getting and Spending Food Stamps

Applications to buy food stamps must be filled out by a member of each applicant household at a food stamp agency, usually located in a county welfare office. A food stamp caseworker processes the application. Receipts are required for certain expenditures, and these expenditures are deducted from a verified report of total household income, to determine the amount of benefits, if any, the household can receive. The caseworker also informs the applicant that employable household members must register for work at the local employment office before the applicant is issued the identification and authorization to purchase (ATP) cards that certify the household's eligibility to buy its stamp quota from an issuance center.

The caseworker's task is simplified if all members of the applicant household are included in a federally aided public assistance grant from AFDC or Supplemental Security Income (SSI). By federal statute, these public assistance households are automatically eligible for food stamps, and this creates an inequitable standard for program eligibility, since some public assistance households have incomes greater than the maximum allowable for non-public-assistance households. According to unpublished estimates, eliminating categorical eligibility for public assistance households would reduce program subsidy costs by just less than 5%.

Because benefit entitlements can sometimes be computed from information collected for the welfare case file, many counties economize by simultaneously certifying households for public assistance and food stamps. In these counties, the cost of food stamps is deducted from the monthly assistance grant, and arrangements are made to mail the stamps to the household along with the welfare check.

Non-public-assistance recipients and households living in counties without mail issuance of stamps must take their ATP cards to a stamp vending office. These offices are often located in banks or post offices, and their services are provided on contract with local food stamp agencies. The times during which stamps are sold vary, depending on the locality. Although federal regulations require that stamps must be sold at least twice a month, many food stamp agencies sell stamps much more frequently. Unfortunately, the Department of Agriculture does not collect data that would enable a statistical summary of these aspects of food stamp sales.

Once the stamps have been purchased, they can be spent on any domestic or imported food item in stores that meet USDA standards for handling the stamps. However, if the household is composed of persons 60 years of age or older and has no cooking facilities, it may use food stamps to buy home-delivered meals from a nonprofit meal delivery service, or elect to purchase meals prepared for the elderly in communal dining facilities. Drug addiction and alcoholic treatment centers may also receive food stamps on behalf of their eligible residents.

A number of regulations protect the right of eligible persons to receive the benefits to which they are entitled under the Food Stamp Act. Within 30 days after a food stamp application is received, the food stamp agency must notify the applicant of its decision to certify or deny program eligibility. (During the 1974–1975 recession, when food stamp applications surged, many food stamp agencies failed to comply with this requirement due to staffing problems.) Upon applying for the program, applicants are informed, in writing, about the hearing procedures by which the household may dispute the agency's decision on eligibility, or contest the amount of benefits designated for the household. Ten days advance notice is prescribed before any action can be taken to reduce or terminate the benefits of a certified household. Extensive safeguards are provided to ensure that persons disagreeing with an agency decision have the opportunity for a fair hearing, including the right of appeal to a final administrative decision by the state food stamp authorities. When the hearing authority finds either an improper denial of program eligibility or an overcharge for stamps sold to the household, there is a stipulation of credit for lost benefits or a refund for any overcharge.

Periodically, food stamp users must repeat the entire food stamp application process, in order to become recertified as eligible to buy food stamps. The time between applications is called the certification period, which conforms to calendar month durations whenever possible. Food stamp certification periods for public assistance households are for the duration of their welfare grant. Ordinarily, non-public-assistance households are certified for 3 months. Exceptions depend on the stability of household income and composition. Shorter periods of eligibility are dictated when there is a possibility of change in income or household status, such as for migrant workers during the work season. On the other hand, certification periods as long as 6 months are allowed when the food stamp agency determines that changes are unlikely. Finally, 1-year certification periods are permitted for unemployable persons with very stable incomes, or for households with readily predictable income from self-employment, provided the food stamp agency also expects no change in composition for either type household.

When any change in household income or deductible expenditures exceeding $25 occurs during a certification period, the household must notify the food stamp agency within 10 days. Actions to adjust eligibility or benefits accordingly are then required of the food stamp agency, and must be reflected in a revision of the purchase price of the stamps bought by the household in its next regular purchase. Similar revisions are necessary when household size changes.

From estimates generated for a sample of non-public-assistance recipients, Wendell Primus (1977) found the mean length of time a food stamp recipient stayed on the program in 1975 was about 7.5 months. Among households with members registering for work, the average stay on the program was 4.8 months; for elderly households, the figure was 15.8 months. For welfare recipients, one would expect to find even longer average stays on the program because welfare income is often more stable than that of other sources; that is, fewer recipients would leave the program due to a rise in income above the eligibility limit.

Food Stamp Means Test

The means test for food stamp eligibility requires that program applicants demonstrate that their household resources do not exceed either of two maximums, one for assets and one for net income. The asset maximums apply to households of every size, but net income maximums increase with household size to register rising household needs.

Some important components of household wealth are not counted as assets for determining program eligibility. The home, one car, household and personal goods, insurance policies, pension funds, and any property essential to self-support are specifically excluded from the list of countable resources. Extra cars or recreational vehicles are counted as assets, along with financial assets such as cash, bank accounts, stocks and bonds, and nonrecurring lump-sum payments. If the total value of these countable liquid assets exceeds $1500 (or $3000 when two or more household members are over age 65), the household is denied eligibility for food stamps. It is estimated that food stamp eligibility would jump 20% if the assets test were eliminated and income were the only means test (Bickel and MacDonald, 1975).

The countable net income definition for food stamp eligibility determination is quite complicated, since many deductions from total household income are permitted. In-kind income, loans, nonrecurring lump-sum payments, and all the earnings of children under 18 years of age do not enter the computation of net income. For purposes of that computation, gross income is restricted to earnings of all adult household members, all returns from assets or self-employment, and any cash payments from welfare programs, pensions, veteran's benefits, farm subsidies, Workers' Compensation, Unemployment Compensation, scholarships, or training subsidies. Then, a host of deductions are subtracted from gross income to determine household net income. Deductions include 10% of wages and salaries (not to exceed $30 a month), income taxes, Social Security taxes, union dues, and any other mandatory payroll deductions. There are further deductions for all medical expenses when they are in excess of $10 a month, payments for child care when necessary for a household member's employment, tuition and educational fees, and unusual expenses like funerals. Finally, there is a deduction for all shelter costs (rent, utilities, and one telephone for renters or property taxes and mortgage payments for homeowners) in excess of 30% of gross income minus all other deductions.

The intent of this definition of net disposable income is to provide a standard for determining need for food stamp benefits that takes into account the various circumstances under which gross income is a misleading indicator of ability to acquire nutritional diets. To illustrate, the shelter deduction may partially account for cost-of-living differences associated with housing. Variations in local tax rates are also neutralized, as are the special needs of households with either extraordinary medical expenses or child care payments that permit a parent to work.

A substantial portion of total program administrative costs is directly attributable to this complicated process of determining eligibility and benefits. Food stamp caseworkers devote considerable time to the calculation of net income, both because there are so many deductible items and because proof of each one must be examined. The likelihood of payment errors undoubtedly increases when complicated calculations are used.

As the number of food stamp applicants rose, these certification costs received more and more attention. In 1976, there were congressional proposals to revise the net income definition by incorporating a standard deduction from gross income. (These proposals are discussed in Chapter 7.) A USDA survey of food stamp households in September 1975 found that 82% of all households claimed deductions, and that the average deduction for all households was $77 (Forscht and Platt, 1976). Deduction amounts were positively related to gross household income, and inversely related to the age of the household head. Deductions increase nonlinearly with household size and level off at about three to four persons per household and then decline somewhat thereafter. Therefore, if a standard deduction were to be set near the overall average, there would be a redistribution of benefits away from larger households toward smaller (often elderly) households. In addition, itemized deductions vary greatly among regions of the country for households with similar incomes. For example, for households with gross incomes below the official poverty line, deductions averaged about $55. By region, the averages for these officially poor households were Mid-Atlantic, $52; Southeast, $55; Midwest, $52; Far West, $68; West-Central, $45; New England, $82 (Congressional Budget Office, 1976). Undoubtedly, this variability is partly due to varying shelter costs among regions.[2] Since below average deductions are observed for officially poor households outside New England, setting a standard deduction at the overall average would favor poor households, but at the expense of redistributing benefits from poor households in the Northeast to poor households in other regions. Tradeoffs such as this demonstrate there are some difficult equity questions raised by proposals for a standard deduction. Moreover, the amount of the deduction (standard or itemized) determines the maximum net income for program eligibility.

---

[2]Regional variation in the shelter deduction is documented by J. Peskin (1975). This paper also provides an excellent discussion of alternatives to the current shelter deduction, and their policy implications.

TABLE 2.1

A Comparison of Poverty Thresholds and Annualized Net Income Maximums for Food Stamp Eligibility for 1975

| Family size | Maximum net income for food stamp eligibility[a] | Poverty line[b] | |
		Nonfarm	Farm
1	$2,520	$2,590	$2,200
2	3,480	3,410	2,900
3	5,040	4,230	3,600
4	6,480	5,050	4,300
5	7,560	5,870	5,000
6	8,640	6,690	5,700
7	9,720	7,510	6,400
8	10,800	8,330	7,100
9	11,520	9,150	7,800
10	12,600	9,970	8,500

[a]Computed from USDA, Food and Nutrition Service (1975).
[b]Computed from Community Services Administration (1975).

Food stamp net income maximums are related to the official gross income poverty line in Table 2.1. This comparison reveals that the food stamp eligibility lines are above the official poverty lines.

BENEFIT DETERMINATION

The benefit schedule of the Food Stamp Program specifies the amount of free bonus stamps a household is entitled to, depending on both household size and household net income. Since 1971, households have had the option of selecting quarter-fractions of the bonus, under a provision known as variable purchase. After examining the general structure of the benefit schedule, the variable purchase option will be explained.

The top row of the benefit schedule shown in Table 2.2 displays food stamp allotments, which are the maximum amount of bonus stamps available to households in the lowest net income bracket. The National Academy of Sciences—National Research Council Recommended Daily Allowances (RDA) of nutrients for persons in various sex—age categories provides the nutritional basis for the monthly stamp allotments. The USDA Consumer and Food Economics Institute used these RDAs to develop an

TABLE 2.2

Food Stamp Benefit Schedule for January–July 1977

Monthly Coupon Allotments and Purchase Requirements—48 States and District of Columbia

	For a household of—							
	1 person	2 persons	3 persons	4 persons	5 persons	6 persons	7 persons	8 persons
	The monthly coupon allotment is—							
	$50	$92	$130	$166	$198	$236	$262	$298
Monthly net income	And the monthly purchase requirement is—							
$0–19.99	0	0	0	0	0	0	0	0
$20–29.99	1	1	0	0	0	0	0	0
$30–39.99	4	4	4	4	5	5	5	5
$40–49.99	6	7	7	7	8	8	8	8
$50–59.99	8	10	10	10	11	11	12	12
$60–69.99	10	12	13	13	14	14	15	15
$70–79.99	12	15	16	16	17	17	18	19
$80–89.99	14	18	19	19	20	21	21	22
$90–99.99	16	21	21	22	23	24	25	26
$100–109.99	18	23	24	25	26	27	28	29
$110–119.99	21	26	27	28	29	31	32	33
$120–129.99	24	29	30	31	33	34	35	36
$130–139.99	27	32	33	34	36	37	38	39
$140–149.99	30	35	36	37	39	40	41	42
$150–169.99	33	38	40	41	42	43	44	45
$170–189.99	38	44	46	47	48	49	50	51
$190–209.99	38	50	52	53	54	55	56	57
$210–229.99	40	56	58	59	60	61	62	63
$230–249.99	40	62	64	65	66	67	68	69
$250–269.99		68	70	71	72	73	74	75
$270–289.99		72	76	77	78	79	80	81
$290–309.99		72	82	83	84	85	86	87
$310–329.99		72	88	89	90	91	92	93
$330–359.99			94	95	96	97	98	99
$360–389.99			102	104	105	106	107	108
$390–419.99			111	113	114	115	116	117
$420–449.99			112	122	123	124	125	126
$450–479.99				131	132	133	134	135
$480–509.99				140	141	142	143	144
$510–539.99				142	150	151	152	153
$540–569.99				142	159	160	161	162

TABLE 2.2 *(Continued)*

Monthly Coupon Allotments and Purchase Requirements—48 States and District of Columbia

	For a household of—							
Monthly net income	1 person	2 persons	3 persons	4 persons	5 persons	6 persons	7 persons	8 persons
	The monthly coupon allotment is—							
	$50	$92	$130	$166	$198	$236	$262	$298
	And the monthly purchase requirement is—							
$570–599.99					168	169	170	171
$600–629.99					170	178	179	180
$630–659.99					170	187	188	189
$660–689.99					170	196	197	198
$690–719.99						204	205	207
$720–749.99						204	215	216
$750–779.99						204	224	225
$780–809.99						204	225	234
$810–839.99							220	243
$840–869.99							226	252
$870–899.99							226	258
$900–929.99								258
$930–959.99								258
$960–989.99								258
$990–1,019.99								258

Source: U.S. House of Representatives (1976).

Economy Food Plan, the cost of which determined stamp allotments from 1964 through 1975. In 1976, the Thrifty Food Plan replaced the Economy Plan as the basis for stamp allotments. The Thrifty Food Plan updates the Economy Food Plan, accounting for recent changes in the National Academy's recommendations, increasing the requirements for certain nutrients for adequate nutrition. Thus the cost for the Thrifty Plan is somewhat greater than that for the Economy Plan. However, aside from their somewhat different bases with respect to specific nutrient requirements, both diet plans were developed in essentially the same manner: After determining which urban households from a 1955 survey comprised the lowest food costs per person quartile, the food consumption patterns of these households were analyzed to discover dietary deficiencies. Then a revised food consumption pattern that would satisfy all RDAs was prepared by changing the mix of habitually consumed foods, such that total costs per person would increase very little. This was accomplished by substituting lower-priced foods with the same nutritional value for some higher-priced ones (for example, red meat and bread both provide iron).

To estimate costs, the families following the food plan are assumed to select the kinds and amounts of foods in the food groups that the urban survey households selected on average. In updating the plan's costs, food prices collected routinely by the Bureau of Labor Statistics are weighted by the average amounts specified for each age—sex category.

For administrative convenience, USDA ties all food stamp allotments to the U.S. average dollar cost of the plan for a family of four with school children, which was $161 in May 1975. Hence the monthly food stamp allotment during July—December 1975 was set at $162 for all four-person households. The stamp allotments for households of all other sizes were also computed from a base of $162, with adjustments for consumption economies of scale, which occur when larger households purchase in quantity or share costly goods, such as housing. For instance, the following formula was used to adjust for the estimated 10% increase in per person food expenditures for a two-person household relative to a four-person household:

$$\$89.10 = (162/4)\,(2) + (.10)\,(162/4)\,(2).$$

For the latter half of 1975, the two-person stamp allotment was $90.

A criticism of the method by which USDA converts the cost of RDAs for individuals into household-size specific stamp allotments is that households of the same size do have differing sex—age composition. Because RDAs differ among sex—age categories, the implication of this criticism is that the actual cost of a diet supplying RDA for all the members of some households may exceed the food stamp allotment for that size household. Although this procedure is administratively convenient, it could conceivably prevent certain households from purchasing a nutritionally adequate diet with their stamp allotments.

In June 1975, a United States Court of Appeals in Washington, D.C. ordered the USDA to devise a new coupon allotment system, pursuant to the court's findings that USDA stamp allotments based on the existing Economy Food Plan did not take account of the varying needs of families, according to the age and sex of their members, or the region of the country in which they live. In *USDA* v. *Rodway,* the court also addressed the issue of administrative convenience:

We agree that there is room for administrative convenience and necessity in the administration of the food stamp program. . . . But we do not think that justifies automatically ignoring generalized,· easily quantified, and easily verified differences among recipients under the rubric of administrative necessity [1975, 514F D.C. Cir].

In response to the Rodway decision, the Department of Agriculture issued regulations describing the procedure for computing stamp allotments, based on the cost of the new Thrifty Food Plan that had been developed independently of the Rodway case. Apparently, the court was satisfied with this reponse from the Department of Agriculture.

Households above the lowest net income bracket must pay a purchase price for their stamp allotment that is less than the redemption value of the allotment but that rises with each net income bracket. Consequently, as net income increases, the food stamp bonus falls until it becomes zero. The net income at which the bonus becomes zero is also the maximum allowable for eligibility. All these points can be illustrated with the help of Table 2.2. Under three-person households, the monthly coupon allotment is $130. Households with net incomes below $30.00 a month receive this entire allotment without spending any of their own cash. The same size household in net income bracket $120–129.99 must pay $30, reducing the bonus amount to $100. Once net income rises above $450 the household becomes ineligible for bonus food stamps.

Figure 2.1 demonstrates how benefits fall as net income increases. Over the entire range of eligible net incomes, the rate at which benefits decline is roughly 30% of each additional net income dollar, as indicated

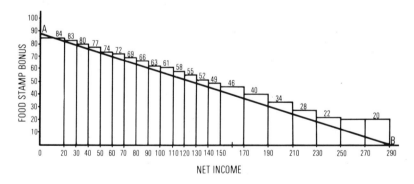

Figure 2.1. *Food stamp bonus for net income brackets, two-person households. From U.S. Department of Agriculture (1975).*

by the slope of line AB. However, it should also be noted that the benefit reduction rate for shifts between certain income—household-size brackets is less than 30% (see Table 2.2).

By federal statute, food stamp allotments are increased every 6 months to maintain the purchasing power of bonus food stamps. The size of each increase is tied to food price inflation, as measured by semiannual changes in the Bureau of Labor Statistics Food Price Index. (During periods of continuous food-price inflation, changes in the size of the allotment do not become effective until 6 months after the end of the period over which the rate of inflation is measured.) Because purchase prices remain constant, the maximum allowable income for eligibility and therefore the brackets below it also rise every 6 months.[3]

Table 2.3, which is based on a four-person household helps to illustrate recent relationships among food-price inflation (as measured by the Consumer Food Price Index), overall inflation (as measured by the Consumer Price Index), food stamp allotments, the food stamp net income maximum for program eligibility, and the official poverty line. During the latter half of 1973, the Consumer Food Price Index increased at an annual rate of 20.7%. As required by law, the first-half of 1974 monthly food stamp allotment was therefore increased from $116 to $143. On an annual basis, this increase implied a new allowable net income maximum of $5676, rising from $4644. Thus the 1973 food-price surge caused the food stamp net income maximum to jump by over $1000. In contrast, over the same period, the annual official poverty line rose only $265, from $4275 to $4540. The official poverty line is indexed by the entire Consumer Price Index (CPI), which increased at less than half the annual rate for the Food Price Index. Thus the relationship between program eligibility and the official poverty line depends on the impact of inflation on food prices, as opposed to prices of other goods.

The variable purchase option adds yet another dimension to the food stamp benefit schedule. This option allows food stamp users to buy any quarter-fraction of their food stamp bonus, and was designed to satisfy program critics who believed that many eligible households failed to use

---

[3]Purchase prices in the benefit schedule are fixed at constant dollar amounts. However, any inflation-induced rise in itemized deduction from gross income also moves recipients into lower net income brackets. Hence individual recipients might actually pay lower constant dollar purchase prices for their stamps as inflation progresses. Thus the combined influence of inflation on bonus stamp payments stems from three sources: increased allotments; reduced purchase prices for those individuals who report increased itemized deductions; and inflation's impact on gross money incomes.

TABLE 2.3
Price Indices, Food Stamp Allotments and Net Income Maximums, with Official Poverty Lines, 1971–1976

Calendar year and quarters	Annual percentage rate of change Food Price Index	Annual percentage rate of change Consumer Price Index	Four-person household					
			Food stamp allotment Monthly	Food stamp allowable net income maximum		Official poverty line	
				Monthly	Annual	Annual	
1971:I&II	3.2	4.0	$108	$360	$4320	—	
1971:II&IV	3.8	3.6	108	360	4320	—	
1972:I&II	4.2	3.0	108	360	4320	$4137	
1972:III&IV	4.7	3.6	112	373	4476	4137	
1973:I&II	16.2	5.9	112	373	4476	4275	
1973:III&IV	20.7	9.2	116	387	4644	4275	
1974:I&II	14.7	10.6	142	473	5676	4540	
1974:III&IV	9.2	12.9	150	500	6000	4540	
1975:I&II	8.0	8.3	154	513	6156	5046	
1975:III&IV	7.9	7.3	162	540	6480	5046	
1976:I&II	—	—	106	533	6636	5485	

Source: Hoagland (1976, p. 21).

food stamps because the full purchase price was too high for their already limited budgets. Before the option became available in 1971, potential food stamp users had to decide each month, whether to buy all or none of their bonus stamps. Clearly, the Food Stamp Program could not help eligibles if they chose not to earmark a sizable proportion of their budget for food. To help offset the possibility that eligibles would not take advantage of the program, variable purchase regulations also allow recipients to buy stamps twice a month. Thus every 2 weeks, all food stamp households can buy one-quarter, one-half, three-quarters, all, or none of their entire monthly food stamp bonus, subject to the constraint that the total purchase in any one calendar month may not exceed the entire monthly bonus. For example, referring to Table 2.2, a three-person household having $30–39.99 in monthly net income choosing to buy one-quarter, then three-quarters, of the allotment would first pay $1 to get $32.50 in bonus stamps; and then 2 weeks later pay $3 for the remaining $97.50 of the $130 allotment.

Available data suggest that the variable purchase option is used by only about 6% of recipient households (Congressional Budget Office, 1976). This low usage may be a result of some food stamp agencies simply failing to inform their caseload that this option is available, which, by federal law they must do. Also, recipients who do not desire to buy the entire stamp allotment every month may drop out of the program from month to month, thereby reducing their total expenditure for stamps without using variable purchase. Another complication arises from the need to control the administrative costs of the program. All households choosing not to buy any stamps in 3 consecutive months lose authorization to purchase, and must be recertified.

Defining the Recipient Unit

Individuals can qualify for food stamps only on the basis of their membership in a household that is eligible for the program. Federal law defines a food stamp household as a group of related or unrelated individuals who are not residents of an institution or boarding house, but are living as one economic unit sharing common cooking facilities and for whom food is customarily purchased in common. The regulations say an "economic unit" is any arrangement by which common living expenses are shared to provide for the basic needs of all members without regard to who earns the unit's income or owns its resources. Despite reference to a group of persons, this definition does not preclude eligibility for single persons who maintain their own household.

By stipulating eligibility for economic units, these regulations differentiate membership in a food stamp household from residence in a dwelling unit. More than one food stamp household can occupy the same living quarters. If some co-tenants take care of their own personal expenses or buy and cook their own food, they can qualify as a separate household. An important implication of this possibility is that some co-tenants can be eligible for food stamps, whereas other are not. In the past, program regulations did imply that unless every member of a dwelling unit was eligible, none could be. A USDA directive stated: "persons who share common living quarters and share the expense for such quarters shall be considered a household [USDA, 1974]. In compliance, food stamp agencies denied eligibility to persons who shared rent payments with ineligible persons. In February 1973, the U.S. District Court for northern California permanently enjoined USDA from such practice, because it conflicted with the regulation that defined economic unit (which does not limit living expenses to rent payments) and because in no case can a group be a "household" unless it shares common cooking facilities and purchases food in common (*Knowles* v. *Butz* 1973, 358 F. Supp. 228).

In 1971 Congress also attempted to bar communes permanently from using food stamps, by redefining "household" to include only groups of related individuals. But in May 1972, a U.S. District Court ruled in favor of plaintiffs Moreno *et al.,* who sought relief from enforcement of this amendment. The court held that the redefinition of household denied equal protection under the law, because a statutory classification was being applied to persons other than those whom Congress had intended to exclude. For example, Plaintiff Jacinta Moreno was a 56-year-old diabetic who lived with a Mrs. Sanchez and the three Sanchez children (*Moreno* v. *USDA,* 1972, 345 F. Supp. 310).

The generality of the household definition also permits striking workers to receive food stamps during those months in which their resources are below the allowable maximums. For example, during the 1971 United Auto Workers strike, many strikers obtained food stamps, to the chagrin of their opposition. Ordinarily, strikers constitute a very small proportion of the program's caseload. The August 1975 Current Population Survey conducted by the Bureau of the Census found .2% of the food stamp households contained a striker (U.S. Senate, 1976).

The use of food stamps by strikers probably does create an incentive to prolong strikes, since the stamps help to alleviate the need to return to work. Thus employers have lobbied to deny strikers food stamps, arguing that the stamps destroy the balance required to maintain collective bargaining. Nevertheless, in June 1974, the House of Representatives rejected an amendment to this effect, 169 to 147. Apart from union pressure, this outcome can perhaps be explained by the desire to protect workers' families, even at the possible cost of substantial loss in economic output from lengthier strikes.

College students are the one group whose food stamp eligibility depends on the characteristics of a household other than their own. According to the USDA, only 1.3% of all stamp recipients in September 1975 were college students. If a student over age 18 is enrolled in an institution of higher education and is properly claimed as a dependent for federal income tax purposes by a taxpayer who is a member of an ineligible household, that student is also ineligible. A congressional amendment to this effect became effective in January 1975, reflecting a long-standing public desire to prevent students from substituting food stamps for alternative sources of support, particularly from nonneedy parents (Federal Register, 1975).

The current law to prohibit certain students from the program was tailored to replace a 1971 amendment that was struck down by the Supreme Court in 1973 because it violated the equal protection and due process guarantees of the 14th and 5th Amendments. The offending amendment, aimed at students, stipulated that

> Any household which includes a member who has reached his eighteenth birthday and is claimed as a dependent child for federal income tax purposes by a taxpayer who is not a member of an eligible household, shall be ineligible to participate in any food stamp program established pursuant to this chapter during the tax period such dependency is claimed and for a period of one year after expiration of such tax period [Edgar, 1973].

"Assuming legitimacy of the Congressional purpose," the Court's decision in USDA v. Murry (1973, 41 F. Supp. 282) stated, "the amendment wholly missed its target [p. 5101]." In support of this summation, three objections were put forth. It is instructive to examine how current regulations meet each of those objections.

First, the 1971 amendment made entire households ineligible, even if just one member (possibly a nonstudent) was claimed as a tax dependent by an ineligible household. By contrast, the 1975 revision explicitly states that only the individual claimed as a tax dependent is disqualified. Second, the Court found the arbitrary nature of the 1971 amendment to be compounded by the requirement that ineligibility would continue beyond the year for which tax dependency had been claimed. The new law restricts the student's ineligibility to the year in which that person is claimed as a dependent. Third, the old law was faulty in that it denied eligibility to all

persons claimed as tax dependents by ineligible househ
gard to whether said tax dependency was legally justified
father claimed dependency without contributing anythi
dependent's support, the dependent would still be ineli
rent regulations specify hearing procedures to give tax dependents ιιι ᵤₚ
portunity to demonstrate they are not properly claimed, that is, to prove
that the taxpayer provides less than one-half of the student's support
during the taxable year.

An important side effect of the new law is a more complicated application procedure for students. Unless the food stamp agency receives proof that a student's parents are already certified eligible for food stamps, Supplemental Security Income, AFDC, or some other welfare program, the student must supply extensive data on the parent's financial situation, along with the usual information about the resources of the student's own household. Two separate eligibility determinations are required—one for the student and one for the parent.

Work Registration

To prevent persons from relying on food stamps instead of seeking employment, work registration is required of all able-bodied, nonaged adults in a household, excepting persons responsible for the care of children or aged dependents, students, and adults employed at least 30 hours a week. Using information supplied by the food stamp applicant, a food stamp official determines which, if any, members of the applicant's household are employable. Employables are then directed to register for work at a state or local employment office, and to accept reasonable offers of employment, that is, job offers at wages exceeding state or federal minimums, for work consistent with their abilities, at an accessible location, and not in a plant subject to a strike or lock out. (In the case of AFDC recipients, the AFDC program determines employability and administers its own work requirement. No further action is taken by food stamp offices.) The employment office receives a Food and Nutrition Service form (FNS-284) from the food stamp agency, to identify each food stamp work registrant. As a safeguard, the Department of Labor has instructed state employment agencies to see that persons who should be exempt are not referred for work registration. Then the employment office assists its food stamp cases just as it would other unemployed job-seekers. If a food stamp employable does not appear for work registration, or avoids or refuses a reasonable offer of employment after his household's food stamp application receives approval, a report is sent to the food stamp office. The food stamp agency then declares the household ineligible for 1 year. Food stamp offices also receive reports when an employable accepts a job, specifying pay rates, so that the household's food stamp benefits can be adjusted accordingly. Every 6 months, employables must reregister at the employment service, which receives some funds from USDA to help carry out its food stamp responsibilities.

Even without a work test, many households would terminate food stamps when they experience increased employment, preferring self-support to government assistance. Thus work registration presumably influences the program's size and expenditures by assisting recipients to find jobs that result in reduced food stamp benefits (or termination of eligibility when the job causes net income to exceed the allowable maximum). It also discourages applications from persons unwilling to register for work.

One can only guess about the number of eligibles who forego food stamps to avoid work registration. (It may be zero.) Yet there are data on

TABLE 2.4
Summary of Food Stamp Work Registration Activities for Fiscal Year 1973

	Category of household, by actvity			
	Employed		Terminated for noncompliance	Total
	Stamp bonus reduced	Terminated		
Number	16,347	32,645	47,312	96,314
As a percentage of all households affected by work registration	17	34	49	100
As a percentage of all food stamp households[a]	.4	.9	1.3	2.6
Resulting total reduction in monthly bonus payments	$608,023	$2,019,490	$3,360,558	$5,988,070

Source: USDA Food and Nutrition Service (1973).
[a]There were 3.6 million food stamp households in fiscal 1973. These households received bonus stamps worth $2.233 million.

the impact of work-registration terminations and benefit reductions. In fiscal 1973, there were 1.2 million work registrants not on public assistance, who were receiving food stamps. This figure represents 10% of the 12.2 million average monthly number of persons enrolled in the program. During that same fiscal year, 2.6% of all enrolled households had their benefits reduced or terminated because they failed to register for work or obtained gainful employment, for a monthly saving in federal costs of $6 million—about 12% of fiscal 1973 federal costs for food stamp benefits. Of course, due to limited employment opportunities in many areas, many work registrants do not receive job offers.

Table 2.4 provides some details on the effects of work registration requirements in 1972–1973. Apparently the work test is effective, since about the same percentage of households were terminated for failure to comply as lost benefits due to employment. And most effects were concentrated in terminations, because among registrants finding employment, only two-thirds of their households became ineligible.

Barry Evans, Jr. *et al.* (1976) studied a sample of food stamp work registrants in selected cities to determine the effect of registration on employment behavior. In general, they found that "if the work test does have a work encouragement effect, it is small [p. 84]." The authors of this study also emphasized that many work registrants do return to work, but that they do not do so because of the registration—they would have anyway.

MAINTAINING PROGRAM INTEGRITY

Food Stamp Quality Control Procedures

In accordance with uniform procedures, states study a quality control (QC) sample of non-public-assistance households receiving food stamps to establish the extent to which food stamp users are legally eligible to receive them, are receiving the correct allotment, and are charged the correct purchase requirement. Also, a sample of households denied eligibility is reviewed to find out how many of these are incorrectly denied food stamps. The purpose of this sample is to provide a means for identifying sources of error and to provide corrective action to reduce these errors, and thereby to increase program efficiency. Upon selection for the QC sample, a food stamp household must cooperate with QC personnel or forfeit benefits for 1 year. State quality control personnel select case files at random, and then review each case to determine errors. In addition, some of these same cases are reviewed at the regional and federal level.

Because the QC sample is drawn from caseload records for households having different certification periods, there must be some conceptual difficulty in establishing whether or not a preventible error has actually occurred. As mentioned earlier, certification periods are durations of time for which expenses and income are expected to remain constant. Eligibility and benefits are computed for a given certification period. However when QC examines a case for errors, it compares recipient reports of current, actual income and expenditures to the caseworker's forecast of income and expenditures expected over the certification period. Because income and expenditures do change during a certification period, small unavoidable discrepancies will be classified as errors, along with serious errors that could be avoided. This problem is magnified because the QC sample is restricted to non-public-assistance cases (about one-half the caseload), whose income tends to fluctuate more than that of public assistance cases. A better picture of serious errors could be obtained if the QC sample were designed to account for differing certification periods and to include all types of recipients. (There are plans to expand QC to include all recipients in the sample [Feltner, 1975].)

Despite these problems, the QC system does provide some indication of the level and kinds of errors in the program pertaining to non-public-assistance cases. (If and when this system of assessing errors is expanded, a more reliable indication will result.) Table 2.5 presents a summary of information from the state QC samples for July–December 1974. The USDA advises that these figures should be interpreted cautiously, because start-up and staffing problems have impeded QC, and because some food stamp agencies sampled by QC had only operated for about 6 months.

If these figures are reasonably correct, it is obvious that problems exist in the management of the Food Stamp Program. Of the total monthly bonus dollars issued to cases reviewed by QC, 28.5% were issued incorrectly, involving an even greater percentage of the number of cases reviewed. Errors are most concentrated on ineligible cases and on overissuing stamps, but the percentage of underissued cases is not small (10.7) and involves 2.6% of all bonus dollars issued.

The USDA does have the power to correct abuses of the program, to reduce the number of errors in eligibility and issuance determinations. Because either the state agency or the recipient household can be responsible for incorrect payments, the USDA has means of rectifying problems stemming from both of these sources.

TABLE 2.5

Case Characteristics and Types of Error by Administrative Region, July–December 1974

Characteristic	Northeast	Southeast	Midwest	West central	West	Total
Number of states (incl. D.C.)	14	8	10	11	8	51
Average monthly caseload						
Number of households (thousands)	415	690	447	529	285	2366
Percentage	17.5	29.2	18.9	22.4	12.0	100.0
Number of cases reviewed	6588	7607	6301	5762	3416	29,674
Percentage with errors[a]						
Ineligible	18.1	18.5	22.4	11.4	13.3	17.3
Eligible-overissue	29.8	28.8	22.6	24.9	20.1	26.0
Eligible-underissue	13.8	13.6	8.4	7.4	7.8	10.7
Bonus dollars issued to reviewed cases (monthly)	$390,391	$561,048	$344,002	$378,779	$241,065	$1,905,285
Percentage of bonus dollars in error[b]						
Ineligible	17.3	19.2	22.3	13.9	13.1	17.5
Eligible-overissue	10.0	8.6	8.2	7.9	6.4	8.4
Eligible-underissue	3.4	3.1	2.3	1.6	2.0	2.6

Source: Feltner (1975, p. 131).

[a]Ineligible errors do not necessarily reflect households that are not in need of food stamp assistance. They include work registration and procedural errors. For example, if errors due to the absence of work registration are excluded, the ineligible error rate becomes 12.5% compared to 17.3% when they are included.

[b]Bonus dollars underissued are not available for all states. Percentages are based on reported data.

TABLE 2.6

Summary of Gross Negligence Charges

Area	Period	Amount of claim billed to the state	Charge
Washington, D.C.	May—June 1970	$59,853	Issuance and use of $58,600 in duplicate ATP cards; theft and use of ATP cards with a bonus value of $5261
Cook County, Illinois	May—June 1970	230,274	Fraudulent issuance and theft in temporary certification offices that accommodated strikers
Monmouth County, New Jersey	July 1970; February 1973	172,613	Issued minimum purchase ATP cards without obtaining an application or income and residence information; certified applicants using an unapproved self-declaration system
Los Angeles County, California	1973—1975	720,000	Multiple certification errors and poor computer controls with no corrective action
Santa Clara County, California	June—July 1974	216,400	Improper determination of the basis of issuance
Oahu County, Hawaii	May 1974	51,000	Overissurance of bonus coupons, due to staff shortages and inadequate training
Seattle, Washington	1971	20,500	Use of volunteers, nepotism, and a complete disregard of program requirements
Lincoln, Nebraska	April 1975	4,174	Certification procedures for Indian households at the Wounded Knee Trial deemed improper
State of Michigan	1972	17,740	State did not heed FNS warning that instructions to local agencies were not in compliance with food stamp regulations

Gross Negligence

Program regulations define gross negligence as agency noncompliance with the issuance rules, resulting in a loss of federal funds. Gross negligence also includes actions that continue to result in losses of federal funds after warnings to state agencies of the need for corrective action. On nine occasions, after the Food and Nutrition Service (FNS) Office of Audit examined a random sample of certification actions to project the total value of stamps improperly issued in a selected period, the USDA has instituted gross negligence charges. Table 2.6 summarizes the charge, the period at issue, and the amount of the billing.

Claims against Household

Upon determining that a food stamp recipient has fraudulently obtained coupons, the state food stamp agency must demand repayment of the bonus coupons issued. The amount of the state's claim against the household is documented in agency files, and funds collected are remitted to FNS. The total number of these claims and their total value for fiscal years 1972–1975 are presented in Table 2.7. The majority of all claims are due to deliberate misrepresentation of facts, and the figures refer to claims for which collection action was undertaken, but not necessarily completed successfully. Also, during fiscal years 1974 and 1975, 53 cases of fraud by issuance personnel were uncovered, with estimated losses of at least $555,000 (USDA, 1975).

In addition to requiring restitution for food stamps, states are encouraged to prosecute offenders under state criminal statues whenever possible. (However, five areas have no applicable laws: New Hampshire, Delaware, Nevada, Guam, and the Virgin Islands.) Table 2.8 details the

TABLE 2.7
Claims against Food Stamp Households for Overissuances of Food Stamps, Fiscal Years 1972–1975

Fiscal year	Number of claims	Total value of claims
1972	10,565	$2,278,678
1973	10,730	2,661,037
1974	17,480	3,810,877
1975	34,463	5,298,033

Source: Feltner (1975, pp. 151–158).

TABLE 2.8

Successful Prosecutions for Food Stamp Fraud in State and Local Courts, Fiscal Years 1974 and 1975

FNS region	Number of cases	Dollar loss
	Fiscal Year 1974	
Northeast	29	$11,878.25
Southeast	238	117,077.50
Midwest	14	9,680.50
West-Central	222	303,485.91
West	18	18,688.00
Total	*521*	*460,810.16*
	Fiscal Year 1975	
Northeast	12	4,237.00
Southeast	255	130,466.00
Midwest	40	21,207.25
West-Central	293	324,604.76
West	33	7,035.00
Total	*633*	*487,550.01*

Source: Feltner (1975, p. 160).

number of successful prosecutions by region for two recent fiscal years, along with the dollar amount of loss related to the fraud committed by these individuals. Comparing these figures to the claims and losses for all households in Table 2.7 demonstrates that most cases of food stamp fraud are not prosecuted.

Accountability for Cash and Coupons

State agencies are accountable to the FNS for food stamp issuances and inventories and for collecting cash from program participants. The FNS in turn, is accountable to the Treasury Department for cash deposits and issuing stamps to states. Since states accept, store, and protect coupons, as well as issue them, they are financially liable for the loss of coupons or monies collected in the sale of coupons. Often some of these duties are contracted to private companies, but the state remains liable.

Figure 2.2 depicts the process of coupon supply and redemption. After a requisition from the state for coupons, FNS orders coupons from a printer, American Bank Note, who ships them to a state issuance or inventory point. From there, the coupons go to local food stamp agencies for

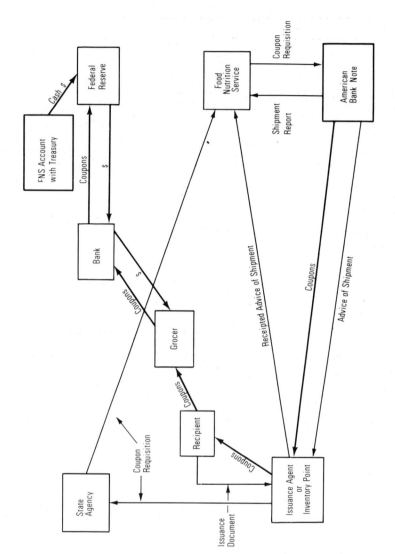

Figure 2.2. Coupon supply and redemption. Feltner (1975, p. 141).

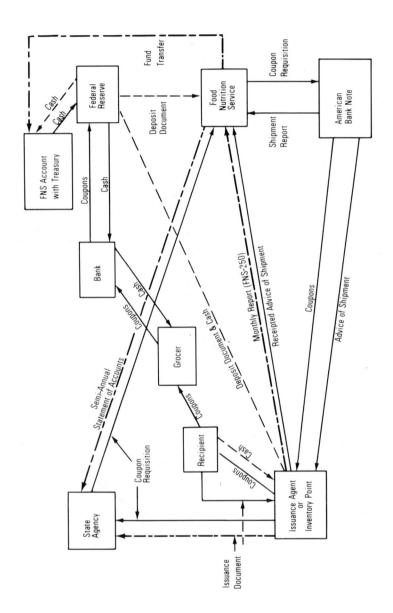

Figure 2.3. Accountability. From Feltner (1975, p. 143).

sale to recipients. Grocers authorized to accept food stamps redeem them for cash at local banks. Then, the food coupons are deposited in the Federal Reserve system, and banks receive cash in return. Thereafter FNS buys the stamps from the Federal Reserve system, via a treasury account. Finally, the stamps are destroyed.

As Figure 2.2 also indicates, the cash collected from recipients for their stamps is deposited in the Federal Reserve system by state agencies. The Federal Reserve system then forwards a deposit document to FNS, for cash paid to the FNS agency account.

Besides the expense of handling and bookkeeping associated with this chain of responsibility, there are costs of establishing the state's accountability. The dashed line in Figure 2.3 illustrates the main components of this accountability system.

Every month, over 6000 state reporting points report to FNS on their coupon inventories, cash deposits, and coupon sales. (Reporting points may be several local food stamp agencies or may represent a statewide operation, such as state mail issuance.) These monthly reports reflect deposits made to FNS; coupon sales activities, that is, coupons authorized, actually sold, and sums outstanding and actually collected; and coupons received, transferred, and issued. Accepting differences between actual and authorized sales as reported, FNS then compares the monthly reports with in-house information such as the previous month's report, shipment reports, receipts for shipments, transfer information, and coupons returned to FNS. Deposit information is compared to deposit documents from the Federal Reserve, for each reporting point. Then on a semiannual basis, FNS prepares a statement of account (see Figure 2.3) that summarizes discrepancies found in the comparisons and reported differences between actual and authorized sales. The monthly reports also allow FNS to determine the amount of funds to transfer from its appropriation to the Treasury Department to cover the bonus value of stamp issuances.

Monitoring Grocers

Through the actions of representatives from 192 field offices, the FNS authorizes and supervises the food stamp activities of retailers and wholesalers. As of July 1975, 249,000 food firms were authorized to accept food coupons, after satisfying a field representative that the firm would serve the program's goals and abide by program regulations. At least once a year, authorized firms are visited by field representatives to advise them of program regulations.

The degree to which regulations are followed is monitored by two methods. There is a computerized system to record the monthly stamp redemptions of all retailers, that compares the volume of stamps with those of the firm's competitors, to spot firms whose excessive redemptions indicate possible wrongdoing. Second, field representatives actively seek out rumors and complaints of retailer violations through contacts with the public, competitors, welfare agencies, and local law enforcement officials. If deemed necessary, there are special compliance visits to the firm in question. Upon a judgment that there is a compliance problem, a letter documenting the suspected violation is sent to the firm. Later the suspect store is monitored by FNS personnel. If voluntary compliance is unsuccessful, the FNS asks the USDA's Office of Investigation to visit the firm. During fiscal year 1975, 684 firms were disqualified for periods from 30 days to 3 years as a result of violations confirmed by these visits. At the discretion of the Department of Justice, 147 firms were prosecuted, resulting in fines up to $3000, periods of probation, and three jail sentences. In addition, 62 firms were disqualified for a 1-year period based on evidence from the computer system that monitors the redemptions of authorized firms. In those instances, the firm's food stamp redemptions exceeded their sales of eligible food items.

In summary, monitoring the program requires quality control, criminal prosecutions, an elaborate accounting system, and periodic checks on food retailers. These activities are expensive, but absolutely essential to maintaining public trust in the program.

This completes the discussion of program regulations and how they are enforced, and we are now ready to analyze the effect of food stamps on recipient consumption behavior. That analysis is presented in the next chapter, which in turn suggests other issues for program evaluation.

3

Food Stamps versus
Cash Transfers

This chapter examines the relative merits of food stamps and cash transfers as methods for assisting low-income households in the context of a societal consensus to provide some form of assistance.

A statement by Lester Thurow (1975) serves as a useful point of departure: "While it is not axiomatically true that cash transfers always dominate restricted transfers, the general economic case for cash transfers is strong enough that the burden of proof should always be on those who advocate restricted transfers [p. 195]." The general economic case Thurow refers to is the principle of consumer sovereignty. Simply stated, this principle is that people know what is best for themselves. Hence Thurow argues that advocates of restricted, in-kind transfers must demonstrate why society ought to interfere with consumer sovereignty by deciding what kinds of goods needy households ought to receive. In the case at hand, food stamp advocates would be required to justify providing stamps intended to restrict consumers to food purchases, instead of providing cash payments allowing unrestricted consumer choice.

There may be valid arguments for the restrictions imposed by in-kind

49

transfers. Perhaps food stamp proponents desire benefits for themselves and for society in general, over and above the benefits accruing to program beneficiaries. These positive externalities might take a variety of forms:

1. Better fed recipients might be healthier and more productive, thereby contributing to the society's general level of well-being through their increased productive contributions. Since the "working poor" are eligible for the program, and because nutritional status affects performance on the job, society's economic output might be increased. In this light, food stamps are seen as an investment with real economic returns for all members of society—an investment that yields greater returns than unrestricted transfers that allow recipients to consume as they see fit.

2. Taxpayer–donors might derive direct satisfaction from increasing food consumption among low-income recipient households, but no satisfaction from increasing consumption in general among these units. Persons favoring nutrition as the key to better living exemplify this motivation for preferring food assistance. Again, this is an externality because nonrecipients as well as recipients benefit.

3. Out of self-interest, certain nonrecipient taxpayers might prefer to assist recipients while stimulating product demand in the food sector of the economy. Because increasing the demand for food benefits nonrecipients participating in every step of the food production and distribution process, the perceived externalities might be quite large.

According to the Food Stamp Act of 1964, the program is intended to strengthen our agricultural economy and to promote nutritional well-being among low-income households. In view of the marked decrease of the farm surplus since 1964, it is difficult to believe Americans continue to favor food stamps primarily as a device to increase agricultural incomes. However, it is easy to demonstrate substantial public concern for the nutritional well-being of the poor. One need only recall the furor that arose in the late 1960s when congressional hearings publicized the discovery of severe malnutrition among rural southern children, or the more recent shock generated by reports that elderly persons resorted to pet food when meat prices skyrocketed in 1973. Nor is it hard to think of reasons for taxpayer opposition to unrestricted cash transfers as a solution to these nutrition problems. When a country-western star receives plaudits for singing "Welfare Cadillac," one can be sure that some taxpayers believe the poor are not to be trusted with unrestricted freedom of choice. However, because purchase of food stamps does not require recipients to buy nutritious foods, one may question whether the program was really intended to promote nutritional status. The idea that taxpayer–donors are aware that the stamps do not require the purchase of nutritional foods suggests that the nutritional goal deserves less emphasis. Instead it may be more accurate to portray food stamps as a program that taxpayers justify on the basis of their desire to promote food consumption because consuming food is thought to be generally beneficial, if not a basic right. And some taxpayers may embrace food stamps out of self-interest—food producers and distributors come to mind.

Whether the public intends food stamps to promote food consumption per se, or to advance nutritional well-being as explicitly stated in the Food Stamp Act, the achievement of either or both goals depends on the extent to which food stamps increase the consumption of food.

To assess program effectiveness in promoting food consumption, we shall compare the effects of food stamps on food consumption to the effects expected for unrestricted cash transfers. The link between the program's impact on recipient food expenditures and nutritional status will be examined in Chapter 4.

Before proceeding, some important considerations affecting the public choice of food stamps versus cash transfers must be considered. If, for whatever reason, a majority of voters overwhelmingly favor in-kind transfers or generally oppose cash transfers, low-income households may actually be better off with food stamps than with stingy (or no) cash transfers. In other words, the cash value of benefits taxpayers are willing to make available to recipients may well depend on what form the benefits take. This interdependence between the amount of income to be redistributed and the form of the redistributive payments can complicate comparisons that are necessary for informed public choice. For this reason, it helps to assume provisionally that society would be willing to transfer cash in dollar amounts equal to the face value of bonus food stamps. Thus to isolate the effects of cash and food stamps on recipients' consumption behavior, the comparisons that follow are between benefits of equivalent dollar cost to the taxpayer.

Another consideration for comparisons between food stamps and hypothetical cash payments of equivalent taxpayer cost is that food stamps require greater administrative expense. Printing, distributing, and accounting for food vouchers is expensive. These extra costs are avoided in a cash transfer program. Other things being equal, taxpayers can economize by providing cash. For the time being, it is necessary to abstract from this fact.

Thus, we maintain the provisional assumption that an alternative to food stamps would be cash payments in amounts equal to the face value of bonus food stamps.

The rate of participation in a food stamp program, as compared to expectations about the willingness of recipients to participate in a transfer program that provides equivalent cash benefits also affects the comparative costs and benefits of the two alternatives. However, the following analysis focuses primarily on program participants. Later, we shall comment on the extent to which the findings of our analysis can be applied to the issue of program participation. These comments provide part of the background for Chapter 6, which studies factors affecting program participation rates.

Finally, the analysis presented in this chapter presumes two audiences, laypersons and economists. Some technical points are only briefly mentioned to facilitate understanding. These points are addressed more completely in Appendix A. Economists are advised to read the next section before Appendix A.

ANALYSIS

An eligible household will participate in the Food Stamp Program if the stamps permit consumption that provides greater satisfaction than goods obtainable without the stamps. It is useful to consider two kinds of consumption behavior on the part of program participants.

Unconstrained Participation

Unconstrained food stamp users consume as they would if they were to receive cash transfers in amounts equal to the face value of their bonus stamps—that is, they devote no greater proportion of their budget to food than they would if they were to receive cash. Clearly, then, recipients who spend more on food than required when spending their full allotment of stamps are unconstrained, because these recipients freely choose to spend more on food than the allotment would require them to buy. We shall refer to these recipients as members of Group I.

An example may help to illustrate the consumption behavior identifying Group I. Consider a four-person household consisting of a married couple and two teenaged sons, spending $175 per month on food, including their $166 stamp allotment. In this case, the household chooses to buy

$9 more food than program participation requires. Hence the program cannot be said to constrain the household's consumption behavior.

When recipients' food expenditures are equal to the face value of the entire stamp allotment, determining whether participation is unconstrained requires knowledge about what the recipients would spend on food if they received cash instead of stamps. Households of this type will be referred to as Group II. If a Group II household would choose to spend only the amount of the stamp allotment on food when it receives a cash transfer equal to the stamp bonus then this recipient household is unconstrained by food stamps. Otherwise, Group II households might be constrained to spend more on food than they would out of an equivalent cash transfer and therefore act as constrained participants.

Constrained Participation

Constrained participation occurs when a household uses food stamps and consequently purchases more food than it would buy if cash were provided instead. As just noted, some Group II households spending only their entire allotment on food may be constrained, because if offered cash in an amount equivalent to their stamp bonus, they might choose to buy less food. However, program rules also permit households to buy less than the full stamp allotment. The variable purchase option permits households to purchase quarter-fractions of the allotment for corresponding quarter-fractions of the full purchase price. And over an extended period, program eligibles may choose to forego part or all of their monthly stamp allotments. Recipients who spend less than the full allotment on food must be constrained by the program; we shall refer to these recipients as Group III. The reason Group III households must be constrained is that they could obtain an even greater food subsidy but choose not to, or do not have the cash needed to buy additional stamps. Presumably these households would gladly take a cash transfer in an amount equal to the bonus, because they could then spend the cash in an unconstrained manner.

Table 3.1 summarizes the discussion of constrained and unconstrained participation. As a first step toward evaluating the effect of the Food Stamp Program on consumption patterns, Table 3.2 presents the percentage distribution of a representative national sample of 1974 recipient households among Groups I, II, and III. From the 1975 interview wave of the Panel Study of Income Dynamics, 833 households who reported receiving food stamps in 1974 were allocated among the three groups by comparing the monthly stamp allotment available to recipients

TABLE 3.1
Summary of Inferences

Recipients' behavior	Type of participation
Group I Food Expenditures exceed the entire stamp allotment	Unconstrained
Group II Food Expenditures are equal to the entire stamp allotment	Unconstrained or constrained
Group III Food expenditures are less than the entire stamp allotment	Constrained

according to household size) during 1974 to estimated monthly food expenditures[1] for these same households (reported annual expenditures on food, divided by 12). According to these comparisons, a surprisingly high percentage of recipient households are unconstrained by the program. Hence, whatever one believes about the ambiguous group (Group II), most households spend more on food than the stamp allotment would require. Allowing for errors in reported food expenditures, a conservative estimate may be that roughly two-thirds of all recipient households are not constrained by the program.[2]

---

[1]For a description of this sample, see J. N. Morgan *et al.* (1972). It is possible that the relatively large size of Group III discovered in the Michigan Panel Data is attributable to involuntary turnover in the recipient population. One could imagine a situation where a household received stamps for a few months while income was transitorily low and received none the rest of the year due to ineligibility; this type of behavior would probably make the Group III population too large as calculated by our methods. A subsample of welfare recipients who also received food stamps was examined, in which fairly stable income and consumption behavior was expected; here too about 70% of the subsample belonged to Group III.

[2]The survey question on food expenditures was:

How much do you (family) spend on food that you use at home in an average week?
$_____ (per week).

A follow-up question asked if the respondent included the extra value of the food (stamp bonus) they got with stamps. According to the survey codebook, about 80% of all stamp recipients did include the stamp bonus when the reported food expenditures. The Michigan Survey Research Center later converted this weekly expenditure amount into an annual value, which was divided by twelve to obtain the desired estimate of monthly food expenditures.

TABLE 3.2
*Percentage Distribution of 1974 Food Stamp
Recipients, by Group (N = 833)*

Group designation	Percentage
Group I (Unconstrained)	71.3
Group II (Unconstrained or constrained)	4.7
Group III (Constrained)	24.0
All recipients *(Total N = 833)*	*100.0*

Source: Panel Study of Income Dynamics (1975).

A better understanding of the effect of food stamps on consumption requires that we also assess the extent to which constrained participants spend more on food than they would out of a cash transfer equivalent to their stamp subsidy. To provide this assessment we estimated the cash equivalent value of food stamps for our 1974 sample of recipient households.

The cash equivalent value of bonus food stamps is the estimated amount of cash that a recipient household would have to receive to feel just as well-off after spending it as it does after spending its bonus stamps. Such values can be derived from information about recipient households and assumptions specifying a hypothetical set of household preferences for food versus other goods. (Appendix A discusses the details of our method, as applied to the 1974 sample households. In addition, the appendix reviews the findings of other studies that estimate cash equivalent values for food stamps.) Once cash equivalent values have been derived, useful comparisons with the stamp subsidies are possible. In particular, it is informative to examine the ratio of the cash equivalent to the face value of the bonus stamps.

If C is the cash transfer amount necessary to make a household indifferent between receiving C and B, the amount of the stamp bonus, then the ratio C/B is the cash equivalent to bonus stamp ratio. By definition, unconstrained recipients would be willing to exchange bonus stamps for cash on a dollar for dollar basis, because for these recipients stamps are no more restrictive than cash. Therefore, the cash equivalent ratio for unconstrained participants is 1. Cash equivalent ratios for constrained participants are less than 1; these participants would value a bonus food stamp with a $1 face value at less than $1 in cash, since they do not desire more food, but would want an increase in general purchasing power.

The value of the ratio indicates the degree to which the in-kind nature of food stamps constrains recipient consumption behavior. In other words, cash equivalent ratios index recipient satisfaction from food stamps, relative to the alternative satisfaction that could be obtained from unrestricted cash transfers in dollar amounts equal to the face value of the food stamp bonus. High ratios indicate relatively greater satisfaction from stamp usage for a given stamp bonus; low ratios indicate relatively less satisfaction. Conversely, because some donors favoring restricted transfers to promote food consumption may want to impose their preference for food on recipients, small cash equivalent ratios correspond to greater satisfaction for these donors. Of course, cash equivalent ratios also indicate the relative effectiveness of stamps, vis-à-vis cash, in promoting food consumption. As cash equivalent ratios rise, the extra food consumption attributable to the in-kind restriction of food stamps declines.

A hypothetical example will help to illustrate this last statement. Suppose we know that a household receiving a $160 monthly stamp allotment would choose to spend $150 in cash per month on food if the household's own cash income were equal to the household's prestamp income plus the cash equivalent value of its bonus stamps. Furthermore, suppose the household pays $100 for the allotment, in exchange receiving bonus stamps worth $60. Assuming this household spends all of its stamps on food during the same month, it will be constrained, because it spends $10 more on food than the hypothetical $150 it would prefer to spend out of an equivalent cash income. This extra $10 of food expenditure is attributable to the use of bonus food stamps. The remaining $50 in bonus stamps is also exchanged for food in a store, but the effect of this exchange is to "free up" $50 in cash that the household would otherwise have spent on food of its own volition; thus $50 of the extra income due to the stamp bonus can be allocated to other goods, although the household might freely choose to spend some part of this extra income on food. To understand why $50 gets "freed up," consider what the household spends out of its own cash on food. It spends $100 for the bonus stamps, and no more. Thus, $50 that would have been used to obtain the preferred $150 in food expenditures becomes general purchasing power. Hence, the cash equivalent value of the $60 stamp bonus is $50, and the cash equivalent ratio is five-sixths, or .833.

Everything we have discussed thus far assumes food stamp recipients use their stamps to buy food for their own use, as intended by program rules. Although these rules clearly forbid the sale of food stamps, some recipients trade part or all of their stamps on the black market for cash in amounts less than the face value of the stamps. The existence of this black market confounds empirical estimation of cash equivalent values for food stamps because there are no reliable data on the characteristics of recipients participating in the black market. Another, entirely legal, method which recipients can use to convert food stamps into cash is to sell food bought with the stamps. Again, we have no reliable data about the extent of this.

In general, ignoring black markets and recipients who sell food tends to bias estimated cash equivalent values downward relative to true values, because recipients can use these methods to relax the constraining effect of the program.

From computations intended to produce a lower-bound estimate, it appears that in 1974 constrained recipient households had an average cash equivalent ratio of about .72. However, after accounting for the cash equivalent ratios of 1.00 for the larger, unconstrained proportion of the recipient sample, the weighted average cash equivalent ratio for 1974 became .92. On average then, about 90 cents of every bonus stamp dollar transferred to recipients is spent as the average recipient sees fit. Conversely, only 10 cents of every bonus stamp dollar is spent on food that the recipient would otherwise choose not to buy. It is also important to note that recipients from small and/or very poor households were found to have cash equivalent ratios substantially below the average value.

As discussed in Appendix A, these findings are fairly consistent with results from previous studies. Still, our estimate does tend to exceed that found in most other studies. For example, Clarkson's (1976) estimate is that 83 cents of every stamp dollar are devoted to general purchasing power. Although all of the studies do differ in estimation procedures, one reason our estimate is somewhat higher is that we were able to determine what proportion of the total sample was unconstrained, whereas most other studies assume that all recipients are constrained to some degree.

It should be emphasized that we have estimated the average cash equivalent value of bonus food stamps actually obtained by program recipients. This value is not necessarily applicable to nonrecipients. It may be that preferences of eligible nonparticipants for food over other goods are systematically different from the preferences of recipients. A policy application of this distinction suggests why it is important.

If the decision not to participate in the Food Stamp Program occurs because cash equivalent ratios are systematically lower for nonparticipants than participants, offering cash instead of stamps might substantially increase the number of participants. If this increase was sufficient to offset the associated decline in average recipient household food consumption due to eliminating the in-kind restriction, total food expenditures under a cash program might exceed expenditures under food stamps. Of course, donors favoring in-kind transfers to boost food expenditures would want to decide whether the expected gain from providing cash would outweigh the added costs of a larger cash transfer program caseload.

SUMMARY AND POLICY IMPLICATIONS

Whether or not food stamp recipients are constrained to buy more food than if they received an equivalent cash transfer depends on household preferences for food versus other goods and on the size and cost of the stamp allotment. In keeping with its food consumption objective, the Food Stamp Program is intended to constrain recipients. However, recipients can minimize the extent to which they are constrained by buying only part of the available stamp bonus. And some recipients freely choose to spend more on food than is made possible by obtaining the entire bonus. Thus, part or all of the subsidy may be substituted for cash expenditures that would have been devoted to food without the subsidy.

Based on empirical evidence from our analysis and other studies, it appears that food stamps do not greatly constrain consumption behavior. In terms of the cash equivalent value of the bonus, the average recipient household can freely choose how to spend most (over 80%) of the stamp subsidy. It is also significant that small and/or low-income households are more constrained than on average. But the main finding is that the naive view that food stamps are restricted, in-kind transfers is largely incorrect, when applied to actual recipient households. Instead, the program primarily provides general purchasing power (although it may be that using stamps would greatly constrain households eligible for, but not participating in, the program). Consequently, the program is much more effective as a provider of income than as a stimulus to the demand for food.

The practical significance of this information depends on what is assumed about the reasons why society has chosen to offer food stamps instead of cash. If food stamps are primarily intended for reasons other than income maintenance, taxpayer–donors could gain by restructuring the program to constrain more recipients, with an associated loss in recipient satisfaction. In other words, to satisfy donors desiring increased food consumption, we would have to force recipients to do what they do not want to. Another possibility is that the public realizes the stamps provide general purchasing power, and yet maintains the program as a political compromise between proponents of income maintenance and others, who prefer to tie aid to food needs. Attempts to constrain more recipients would endanger this compromise. On the other hand, if unrestricted income transfers have become more popular, the recognition that food stamps are "near cash" transfers might provide part of the impetus for replacing the stamps with equivalent cash payments, or for restructuring the program to relax the constraints on those small and/or very low-income households that are now relatively constrained. Furthermore, it must be remembered that our main conclusion does not necessarily apply to eligible nonparticipants. Depending on their reasons for not using the stamps, these eligibles may systematically value food stamps less highly than participants. Relaxing program constraints might, therefore, induce increased participation.

4

Nutritional Effects of Food Stamps and Experimental Cash Transfers

This chapter reviews existing evidence on the nutritional effects of the Food Stamp program. Because the evidence is sketchy, a study of the effect of experimental cash transfers and nutritional adequacy is also discussed. Of course both cash and food stamp subsidies increase purchasing power. Therefore, we begin with an overview of the general relationship between nutritional adequacy and household income in the United States. We then posit a simple model of the nutritional achievement process to facilitate the discussion of relevant empirical studies. A final section displays some measures of nutritional cost-effectiveness, that lead to some policy conclusions.

INCOME AND NUTRITION

A national sample suitable for examining the relationship between income status and nutritional well-being was conducted in 1971 and 1972 by the National Center for Health Statistics of the Department of Health

Education and Welfare (1974). This Health and Nutrition Examination Survey (HANES) collected measures of nutritional status for a sample representing the United States' civilian, noninstitutionalized population aged 1–74 years. The Bureau of the Census cooperated in the sample design and initial interviews, and special field teams including professional and paraprofessional medical and dental examiners, along with technicians and other staff, conducted the examinations of sample persons at mobile examination centers. In addition to information on nutrient intakes, HANES also collected data on socioeconomic characteristics of interviewees, affording nutritional comparisons among age, race, sex, and income groups. The published HANES tables restrict income comparisons to two groups—persons living in households with income below the official poverty level and those in households above it. As is appropriate for the official poverty definition, total household income for the last 12 months was recorded, including total cash income from any source, but excluding payments in-kind, such as food stamps. These income values provided the numerator for the poverty income ratio. The denominator was a multiple of the total income deemed necessary to maintain a family of given characteristics on a nutritionally adequate diet, as constructed from the Department of Agriculture's Economy Food Plan. This denominator adjusts the income maintenance requirements by family size (incorporating scale economies), sex of family head, age of the head in families with one or two persons, and farm–nonfarm residence. When the household's poverty income ratio exceeds 1.0, that household's income is above the poverty threshold; when less than 1.0 it is below. For example, if a male-headed farm family of four persons had 1971 income less than $3528, this family was listed among the "below poverty income level" households. In reviewing the HANES results, it should be remembered that some food stamp eligibles are in the above-poverty income group.

A substantial proportion of all persons surveyed were found to have low caloric intakes. In both the below- and above-poverty-line income groups, intakes of less than 1000 calories were found for an average of about 14% of the white children aged 1–5 years, and about 23% of the black children of the same age and income statuses. Similarly, in both income groups, respectively, 20% and 36% of whites and blacks over 60 years of age had caloric intakes of less than 1000 calories. Hence, although calorie deficiencies do vary by age and race, they are found in both poor and nonpoor income groups. With respect to protein intake, the HANES summary reported little variation by race or income within most age groups, as measured by average protein intake per thousand calories.

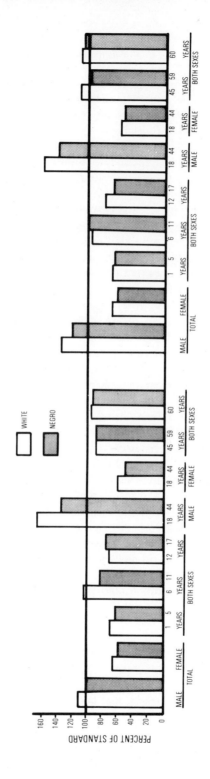

Figure 4.1. Mean iron intake as a percentage of standard by age, sex, and race for income levels, United States, 1971–1972. From U.S. Department of Health, Education, and Welfare, National Center for Health Statistics (1974).

Based on these findings, one can conclude that income level does not substantially affect the intake of nutrients supplying energy and growth for members of most U.S. households.

In examining the results for calcium, iron, vitamin A, and vitamin C, however, a different conclusion emerges. There are nutritional deficiencies among both officially poor and nonpoor households, but in most instances, these deficiencies are greater among the officially poor. With only four exceptions, mean intake of nutrients, as a percentage of the RDA for calcium, iron, vitamin A, and vitamin C, was lower for the poor than for the nonpoor in all age−race−sex groups (National Academy of Sciences, 1974). Yet with the exception of calcium intake for black and white children of both sexes aged 1−5 years, more than 30% of persons in *both* poor and nonpoor groups always had nutrient intakes below the RDA. The most serious deficiencies by far were recorded for iron intake. Even the mean intake for most groups does not exceed the iron standard, poor or nonpoor. Based on biochemical tests as well as the evidence just discussed, the HANES report concludes there is an iron deficiency at all age levels among both income groups. (See Figure 4.1.)

To summarize, the HANES study shows that nutrient deficiencies were observed for both officially poor and nonpoor households. However, these deficiencies are most serious among the poor, implying that income and nutritional well-being are positively correlated. This inference is supported by evidence from Mohammed Abdel-Ghany's (1974) multivariate analysis of nutrient intake among urban households sampled in the Department of Agriculture's 1965−1966 Household Food Consumption Survey. Controlling for other socioeconomic characteristics, Abdel-Ghany found a positive and statistically significant relationship between household income after taxes and the respective adequacy measures of intake for niacin, ascorbic acid, protein, vitamin A, and iron. This finding supports the general presumption that increasing a household's income has a positive impact on nutritional status. However, in order to evaluate the extent to which income transfers such as food stamps actually alter nutrient intakes, a somewhat more complicated view of the process of nutritional achievement is needed.

FOOD STAMPS AND NUTRITION

The process that determines the nutritional adequacy of a household's diet can be represented by

$$N = (N/E) \ (E/Y) \ (Y), \qquad\qquad (1)$$

where N measures the nutritional intake of the household, E is total expenditure on food, and Y is disposable income. Then N/E is a measure of household nutritional efficiency, units of nutrition per dollar of food expenditure and E/Y is the household's average propensity to consume food. It follows from Equation (1) that an increase in household disposable income will raise the household's nutritional intake. Two versions of this model stem from two behavioral hypotheses about nutritional efficiency. We shall discuss these two versions as they apply to food stamps.

Constant Nutritional Efficiency

In a constant-nutritional-efficiency version of the nutritional achievement model, household disposable income is not related to nutritional efficiency. A change in income affects nutritional intake only insofar as it induces a change in total food expenditure, which is then converted into nutrient intake. As a first approximation, one can interpret the Food Stamp Program's influence on nutritional achievement in terms of constant nutritional efficiency, since the main function of the program is to offer recipients an opportunity to increase food expenditures at reduced cost. The nutritional intake of recipient households is expected to rise solely as a result of change in food expenditure levels. One searches in vain for any aspect of program regulations that is intended to improve nutritional efficiency among recipient households. Yet it may be that nutritional efficiency is altered when households use food stamps, which suggests a second version of the nutritional achievement process.

Variable Nutritional Efficiency

If nutritional efficiency varies with the level of disposable income, changes in income have a dual influence on nutritional achievement. As in a constant efficiency model, an income change would affect food expenditures. Moreover, in a variable efficiency model, a change in household income is expected to influence the efficiency at which food expenditures are converted into nutrient intake. To illustrate, increased income from food stamps might permit the homemaker to take more time and care in meal preparation if the food stamp subsidy allowed a reduction in time spent in market work. In this hypothetical example, nutritional efficiency varies positively with disposable income. However, evidence from the study by Abdel-Ghany (1974) suggests that nutritional efficiency actually decreases as income rises: "The quantities of nutrients obtained per dollar decreased for higher income groups. This suggests that lower income households may have been substituting lower priced and more nutritious foods for more expensive and less nutritious foods consumed by households with higher incomes [p. 132]."

Based on this evidence, one might expect that providing food stamp income actually reduces nutritional efficiency, perhaps even offsetting any positive influence of the increased level of food expenditures on nutritional intake. However, because the program does provide stamps that are intended only for expenditure on food, one cannot rule out the possibility that something about the stamps themselves causes increased nutritional efficiency. For instance, it is conceivable that providing food stamps could focus increased attention on the selection of food items, possibly exerting a desirable influence on nutrient intake.

In order to assess the role food stamps actually play in the nutritional achievement process, we shall review two studies that surveyed food stamp participants and nonparticipants. The results of Sylvia Lane's 1975 survey of Kern County, California households are examined first; this study compares food expenditure amounts and the dietary adequacy of nine important nutrients. Then J. Patrick Madden and Marion D. Yoder's (1972) multiple regression analysis of the determinants of overall nutritional achievement among 1969–1970 rural Pennsylvania participant and and nonparticipant households is discussed. These Pennsylvania results provide evidence about the effect of food stamps on nutritional efficiency because Madden and Yoder held household income and food expenditure levels constant in their analysis.

Food Stamp Effects Observed in Kern County, California

Averages relevant for assessing the monthly impact of the Food Stamp Program on food expenditures were computed separately for 151 food stamp participant and 178 nonparticipant program eligible households residing in Kern County, California. For all practical purposes, the average monthly cash incomes of the two groups were identical. However, the combined cash and in-kind income of participants exceeded that for nonparticipants by about $45 per month because participants' in-kind income averaged $51.02, including $43.70 in bonus food stamps, whereas nonparticipant in-kind income averaged less than $8 per month.

The monthly value of food available to participants also exceeded the corresponding nonparticipant amount by $18 per month, although participants actually spent $25 less of their own cash on food than nonparticipants.

The $18 average increment in food expenditures among participant households was less than half of the additional purchasing power attributable to bonus food stamps, indicating that some income "freed" from allocation to food was spent on other goods and services. This finding is supported by empirical estimates of the cash equivalent value of food stamps, and it has a negative implication for the cost-effectiveness of food stamps in promoting nutritional improvement, because food stamp users do not devote all of their subsidy to food purchases. Still, some nutritional improvement could result from the portion of bonus stamp income that is spent on food, and there is some evidence of this among Kern County households.

Table 4.1 displays percentages of Kern County food stamp eligibles that received 100% of the RDA for nine important nutrients. Household nutrient intakes were measured by the 24-hour recall method, whereby survey respondents report the types and amounts of all foods consumed by household members during the day prior to the interview. Based on these reports, investigators convert quantities of the various foods con-

TABLE 4.1

Percentage of Households with Nutritional Achievement Ratios at 100% of Recommended Daily Allowances, for Food Stamp Program Participants and Nonparticipants, Kern County, California, 1973

Nutrient	Participants (N = 151)	Nonparticipants (N = 178)
Calories	54.3	50.6
Protein	96.7	86.0
Calcium	53.6	51.1
Iron	58.3	60.1
Vitamin A	41.7	44.4
Thiamine	66.2	54.5
Riboflavin	82.6	71.4
Niacin	97.4	96.1
Vitamin C	54.3	56.7

Source: Lane (1975, p. 12).

sumed into nutrient intake measures. It should be emphasized that the validity of these measures depends crucially on the accuracy of the respondents' recall, and that nutritionists disagree about the merits of the 24-hour recall method. However, the working presumption here is that the 24-hour method determines nutrient intake with a degree of accuracy sufficient for valid group comparisons.

According to Table 4.1, less than 85% of both Kern County participant and nonparticipant households obtained the RDA for seven nutrients. Moreover, only about half of both groups obtained the standard for calories, calcium, and vitamin C. Yet there were more participant households at 100% percent of the standards for calories, protein, calcium, thiamine, riboflavin, and niacin than nonparticipant ones. These findings suggest food stamps do have some positive influence on nutritional achievement. However, this evidence is not conclusive, because there may be important differences in the characteristics of participant and nonparticipant households that are unrelated to the food stamp program and yet actually account for the observed difference in nutritional achievement. Taking account of this possibility requires a multivariate analysis incorporating many explanatory variables.

Evidence from Rural Pennsylvania

The study by Madden and Yoder incorporates a number of explanatory variables and addresses the issue of variable nutritional efficiency. That is, in terms of the identity $N = (N/E)\,(E/Y)\,(Y)$, only N was permitted to vary, because participant and nonparticipant households were compared in a multivariate context that held constant income and food expenditure levels. Hence, observed effects on nutritional adequacy that are unique to food stamp users can presumably be attributed to stamp-related variations in nutritional efficiency.

Table 4.2 displays the results of a key regression based on the Pennsylvania data. A simple average of the nutritional achievement ratios observed for 10 nutrients was the dependent variable in this regression, which includes nonparticipants and participants in either commodity distribution or the food stamp programs of Huntingdon and Bedford counties. Two versions of the Food Stamp program are distinguished: FS1 refers to the 1969 program, whereas FS2 is the modified program adopted in April 1970. Food program households were also subdivided according to whether or not food aid was received more than 2 weeks prior to the household interview. All other variables account for differences in access to food and/or its preparation.

TABLE 4.2

A Multiple Regression Analysis of the Nutritional Impact of Food Stamp Usage in Rural Pennsylvania

Variable	Count (n_i)	Regression coefficient (b_i)	Standard error (s_{b_i})	Relevant t-values	F Ratio
Food program status[a]					9.91**
Huntingdon County:					
DSFS1 < 15 days	24	−15.265	14.463		
No FS1 or 15+ days	138	4.687	7.967		
DSFS2 < 15 days	34	−3.074	14.479		
No FS2 or 15+ days	94	19.248	7.636		
Bedford County					
No CD	89	15.873	2.269		
No FS1	112	11.492	2.094		
DSCD < 15 days	66	12.598	9.818		
DSCD 15+ days	97	10.993	2.936		
DSFS1 < 15 days	67	15.411	8.641		
DSFS1 15+ days	36	7.158	3.714		
DSFS2 < 15 days	64	5.369	8.776		
(Omitted: no FS2, Bedford)	157				
Income−Poverty threshold					3.41*
Income/Poverty = 1−1.25	90	1.224	1.903	.64	
Income/Poverty = 1.26+	147	4.549	1.747	2.60**	
(Omitted: Income/Poverty < 1.0)	764				
Monthly food expense/person ($)	n/a	.103	.038	2.69**	
Income frequency (1 = once or less per mo.)	253	−3.538	1.478	2.39**	
Education of homemaker (years)	n/a	−.035	.062	.56	
Age of homemaker (years)	n/a	−.090	.040	2.23*	
Home produced food (1 = yes)	523	2.431	1.106	2.20*	
(Omitted: no HPF)	478				
Size of household					3.16*
3−4	261	1.819	1.649		
5−6	231	5.176	1.885		
7+	202	4.617	1.915		
(Omitted: < 3)	307				
Nutr. Aide visits:[b]					
3−5	37	7.397	6.863		
6−12	57	4.445	7.028		
13−60	29	5.651	7.818		
(Omitted: < 3)	878				
Interactions:					
N.A.V. < 3; HFS < 15 days	32	19.085	12.192		
N.A.V. 3+; HFS < 15 days	24	10.185	14.185		
N.A.V. < 3; no. F.S. or >15 days	135	−.489	7.801		

(continued)

69

TABLE 4.2 (Continued)

Variable	Count (n_i)	Regression Coefficient (b_i)	Standard Error (s_{t_i})	Relevant t-values	F Ratio
N.A.V. 3+; no. F.S. or > 15 days	92	−6.600	10.340		
(Omitted: HFS 15+ days)	718				
Unit Vector (constant)	n/a	70.597	4.565		
Weekdays[c]	932	−2.661	2.117	1.26	
(Omitted: Sat. and Sun.)	69				
Days since payday[d]					1.89
15+ days	198	4.151	3.150		
Not reported	89	−3.218	3.213		
(Omitted: < 15 days	714				
Interactions:					.94
DSBP < 15; CD < 15 days	39	1.713	10.378		
DSBP 15+; CD < 15 days	24	−5.303	10.802		
DSBP < 15; FS < 15 days	151	−3.695	8.811		
DSBP 15; FS < 15 days	33	−3.089	9.372		
DSBP < 15; no F.A.	400	−2.223	2.958		
DSBP 15+ no F.A.	102	−7.107	3.861		
(Omitted: all DSFA 15+)	252				

Source: Madden and Yoder (1972, pp. 54−55).

[a] For example, DSFS1 < 15 days refers to households that received stamps from the 1969 program, less than 15 days prior to the survey interview. Similarly, CD refers to the receipt of commodities, and FS2 refers to the stamp program, as modified in April 1970.

[b] Refers to the total number of visits to the household, prior to the interview.

[c] Day of the survey was expected to have an effect on nutrient intake, because many families customarily have larger meals on weekends, particularly Sunday.

[d] DSBP refers to the number of days since the month's largest pay.

*$p < .05$.

**$p < .01$.

n/a = not available.

$R^2 = .194$.

A.O.V. of regressions: $F = 6.101$**.

Madden and Yoder concluded that the dietary impact of food stamps was significant and positive only under unfavorable conditions, such as more than 2 weeks since payday or receiving food stamps. Perhaps this impact operates through increased nutritional efficiency during temporary cash and food stamp shortages. There was no other evidence that nutritional efficiency varied between food stamp users and nonparticipants.

From a multiple regression analysis of monthly food expenditures per person, Madden and Yoder further concluded that food stamp usage typically does not increase food expenditure, net of the effects of income adequacy and the other control variables. Because income adequacy incorporates the bonus food stamp value, an important implication is that food stamp users in rural Pennsylvania did not purchase more food than nonparticipants at comparable income levels. Since total food expenditure ordinarily rises with income, this implication is not inconsistent with Lane's observation that food stamp recipients spend more on food than nonrecipients with lower average incomes.

Based on the evidence from surveys in Pennsylvania and California it would be hazardous, at best, to conclude that food stamps have a substantial impact on either nutritional efficiency or nutritional achievement. Although the Lane study of California households suggests there may be a positive impact on nutrient intake due to food stamp usage, one cannot rule out the possibility that some factor unrelated to food stamps caused the greater nutrient intakes of food stamp users. With respect to nutritional efficiency, the study by Madden and Yoder failed to find any positive impact of food stamp usage. However, because both studies rely on respondents to recall food intakes of every household member during a 24-hour period, and since these studies are severely restricted geographically, readers may wish to withhold final judgment about program effectiveness until other studies become available.

NUTRITION AND EXPERIMENTAL CASH TRANSFERS

Cash transfers are often advocated as a preferred alternative to food stamps because recipient households may spend cash in whatever way they wish. Since an adequate diet promotes well-being, it can be expected that part of any cash transfer will be spent on nutritious food. Hence, cash payments may improve the nutrient intake of recipient households. O'Connor, Madden, and Prindle (1975) examined the effect of cash transfers on the mean adequacy ratios[1] of Iowa and North Carolina participants in the Rural Negative Income Tax (RNIT) experiment (Bawden, 1970).

---

[1]Because experimental cash transfers might have substantial impacts on nutrients in one direction and offsetting influences in another direction, the use of the average nutritional adequacy ratio as a dependent variable could disguise nutritional effects of the experiment. Thus, O'Connor *et al.* (1975) present results for nutritional adequacy ratios of individual

Since empirical evidence suggests food stamps probably do not compel greater food expenditures than observed for nonparticipants at comparable income levels, one might argue that food stamps are the same as cash, and therefore that the effect of cash payments on nutrition is already known from the survey analysis of food stamps and nutrition. However, there are three reasons for reviewing the RNIT study of nutrition effects. First, the experiment affords comparisons between a cash recipient experimental group and a carefully selected control group of nonrecipients, whereas food stamp nonparticipants may be systematically self-selected for households having markedly different food consumption preferences than those of participants. Second, the experiment paid some households more generous benefits than they would receive from food stamps, extending the range of income levels beyond that observed in the food stamp surveys. Third, inferences about transfer payment effects on nutrition can be stated more confidently when they are drawn from data collected in different locations and time periods. (On the other hand, it should also be noted that the behavior observed in the food stamp surveys may differ from responses to the RNIT experiment, due to the experiment's limited duration.)

The main findings about the effect of experimental cash payments on mean nutritional adequacy ratios are best discussed with the help of the regressions displayed in Tables 4.3 and 4.4. Except for the fact that monthly food expenditures are omitted, the independent variables in those two regressions serve the same purpose as their counterparts in the Madden–Yoder analysis of food stamp effects. An income adequacy ratio (measured net of the cash payment for the relevant quarter of experimental time) controls for prepayment income level, whereas other variables net out the influence of factors thought to affect nutritional efficiency and food expenditure. Therefore the coefficients for second-quarter membership in the experimental treatment group (Table 4.3) and for third quarter RNIT payment amount (Table 4.4) each provide a separate measure of the independent effect of cash transfers on mean adequacy ratios. These coefficients indicate a positive and significant improvement in dietary adequacy in North Carolina, but show no significant influence of cash transfers on the nutritional achievement of Iowa families.

Further analysis of the RNIT data revealed that the improvement in

---

nutrients, which are consistent with those for their ratio averages. Moreover, they truncated all ratios at 100% RDA, to be consistent with the view that gross overconsumption of some nutrients cannot compensate for underconsumption of others.

TABLE 4.3

Estimated Regression Coefficients [a] and t-Values for Mean Adequacy Ratios in Quarter 11 of the Rural NIT Experiment

	Coefficient	t-Value
Program variables		
Treatment Effect Iowa	− .007	0
Treatment Effect N.C.	3.556	2.42
Other variables		
Race, Black = 1	2.696	1.79
Income Adequacy Ratio [b]	.108	.23
Average Equity [c]	6.751	1.52
Home-produced Food	5.005	4.11
Sunday Meals	−3.49	.21
Meals typical	5.609	4.10
Age of head		
Less than 31 years	6.50	2.22
31−50 years	5.23	2.24
51−64	4.24	1.97
Family size		
1−2	1.34	.65
3−4	.66	.39
5−6	1.66	.97
Index of food knowledge		
Scored 0	−9.70	3.54
Scored 1−2	−2.07	1.41

Source: O'Connor *et al.* (1975, p. 59).
[a] Regression constant not reported.
[b] Equals $(Y - NIT)/PL$, where Y is total income, NIT is the negative income tax payment in Quarter 3, and PL is the household's poverty line need standard.
[c] Average equity measures the household's nonhuman wealth.

mean adequacy for North Carolina families stemmed from gains in the intake of those nutrients most often deficient in North Carolina diets. O'Connor *et al.* also found that the overall nutritional level of Iowa families considerably exceeded that of North Carolinians, which the investigators interpret as an indication that the lack of any significant Iowa payment effect could be related to a smaller margin for dietary improvement in Iowa. Cultural differences were mentioned as another explanation.

At any rate, conflicting evidence about the impact of experimental cash payments on nutritional achievement precludes a confident conclu-

TABLE 4.4

Estimated Regression Coefficients [a] and t-Values for Mean Adequacy
Ratios in Quarter 3 of the Rural NIT Experiment

	Coefficient	t-value
Program variables		
NIT pay effect Iowa	− .707	.30
NIT pay effect N.C.	3.328	1.80
Other variables		
Race, Black = 1	−3.868	1.99
Adequacy ratio [b]	− .940	1.25
Average equity [c]	13.706	2.30
Sunday meals	4.036	2.07
Meals typical	9.573	5.07
Age of head		
Less than 31 years	10.18	3.02
31−50	9.55	3.18
51−64 years	8.72	3.02
Family size		
1−2	−3.59	1.39
3−4	.81	.38
5−6	1.19	.56
Index of food knowledge		
Scored 0	−5.80	1.65
Scored 1−2	.05	.03

Source: O'Connor et al. (1975, p. 59).
[a]Regression constant not reported.
[b]Equals $(Y - NIT)/PL$, where Y is total income, NIT is the negative income tax payment in Quarter 3, and PL is the household's poverty line need standard.
[c]Average equity measures the household's nonhuman wealth.

sion that cash transfers are an appropriate mechanism for boosting nutritional levels among all low-income households.

COST EFFECTIVENESS

Estimates of the cost effectiveness of transfer payments for nutritional improvement purposes are presented in Table 4.5, as a prelude to some policy conclusions. The table summarizes the cost and nutritional effect of food stamps and experimental cash payments when the observed nutritional impact of these income transfers was most strong. Under those most favorable conditions, the cost per point increase in the mean adequacy

TABLE 4.5

Nutritional Cost-Effectiveness of the Food Stamp Program and the Rural Negative Income Tax Experiment, under More Favorable Conditions

	Percentage increase in mean adequacy ratio	Average cost per day[a]	Cost per point increase in mean adequacy ratio
		Food Stamps	
Bedford County			
FS1	7.9	$ .89	$ .11
FS2	9.4	1.86	.20
Huntingdon County			
FS1	3.6	.78	.22
FS2	1.3	1.35	1.04
		Rural Negative Income Tax	
Iowa			
Quarter 3	−.43	$5.21	—
Quarter 11	−.01	5.34	—
North Carolina			
Quarter 3	3.02	5.21	$1.73
Quarter 11	3.56	5.34	$1.50

Sources: Madden and Yoder (1972, p. 72); O'Connor *et al.* (1975, p. 84).
[a]Arithmetic mean of federal government cost of average daily transfers received by food stamp participants or cash recipients, excluding administrative costs borne by state and local agencies.

ratio was substantially lower for food stamps. Bonus food stamp costs per day were much less than the per diem cash transfers paid by the RNIT experiment. Hence, although in one instance a most favorable RNIT nutrition effect did exceed a food stamp effect, food stamps were always more cost-effective.

Upon similar comparisons, O'Connor *et al.* concluded that neither cash nor food stamps were particularly cost-effective, relative to almost any direct method of supplementing low-income diets. That is, the cost per point improvement in nutritional adequacy from the hypothetical addition of certain nutritious foods (e.g., milk) to reported dietary intakes is less than 8 cents per day.

SUMMARY AND POLICY CONCLUSIONS

Taking the studies reviewed here at face value, the major finding of this chapter is that food stamps may not be a very effective device for improving diets among low-income households. According to available evidence, programs to deliver cash in amounts provided by the RNIT experiment seem unlikely to succeed where food stamps have failed. Instead, more direct intervention to change the nutritional efficiency of low-income households is needed. A number of programs that might accomplish these changes are already operated by USDA, albeit on a much smaller scale than the Food Stamp Program. They include the Supplemental Feeding Program for Women, Infants and Children, the Special Food Service (Day Care) Program for Children, the School Lunch Program, the School Breakfast Program, and the Special Milk Program. (See U.S. Senate, 1974.)

Perhaps the more interesting implications of this chapter have to do with welfare policy in general. Once it is recognized that the Food Stamp program does not necessarily induce purchases that markedly improve nutritional adequacy, the program's role as a provider of general purchasing power comes into focus. It is hoped that this chapter contributes to the public discussion of that issue by suggesting the extent to which food vouchers actually perform the nutritional task desired by proponents of this particular form of in-kind transfer payment.

5

Food Stamps and the
Income-Maintenance
System

Because food stamps contribute to the resources of low-income persons (among persons participating in the program in 1974, bonus stamp values averaged $151 per year) the program is considered part of the federal income-maintenance system—income-conditioned programs that transfer cash and in-kind income to meet specific needs. Based on characteristics associated with these needs, Congress has defined groups that are eligible for each program. (See U.S. Congress Joint Economic Committee 1975.) Because households have members with different characteristics, and since persons can belong to more than one eligible group, a single household may participate in more than one income-maintenance program. Thus the effect of any one program on household resources and behavior should not be studied as if it were the only program providing assistance to that household.

This chapter examines how the Food Stamp program functions in the context of the entire income-maintenance system. After discussing who gets food stamps, our focus shifts to the problems and advantages that arise when food stamp users also receive benefits from other transfer programs. Then the contribution of food stamps to the resources of these multiple-benefit households is analyzed using the official poverty line as the standard for measuring income adequacy. Finally there is an assessment of the poverty reduction effort of the Food Stamp program.

FOOD STAMPS AND THE POVERTY POPULATION

According to a September 1975 survey of food stamp households (U.S. Senate, Select Committee on Nutrition and Human Needs, 1976) 77% of all recipient households had incomes below the official poverty line, and these poor households obtained 86% of total bonus stamp dollars. Only 9% of all recipient households had incomes exceeding 125% of the poverty line, accounting for about 5% of total program benefits. (In 1975, the poverty line for a four-person family was $5,050; hence 125% of the poverty line was $6313.) Thus, although food stamps contribute to the resources of many near-poor households, the program's benefits go primarily to households below the official poverty line. Moreover, most of the households with incomes exceeding 125% of the poverty line qualify for benefits because of their relatively high work-related expenses.

On the other hand, a substantial proportion of all food stamp households (23%) do have incomes above the poverty line. Appendix B, Table B.1 demonstrates that the demographic characteristics of food stamp recipients in 1974 were roughly similar to those of the poverty population. However food stamp recipients were more likely to live in the central city, and were somewhat less concentrated in the South than the poverty population. In addition, food stamp households were headed by somewhat older persons, and more often by nonwhite persons or females than were poor families. Poor families also average more members than food stamp households, because single, unrelated individuals are counted as households for food stamp purposes. Locational and residential differences between the two populations may be explained by the more highly developed welfare services outside the South, in central cities, and in non-farm areas, which presumably affects access to, and information about food stamp benefits. With respect to household type, elderly, nonwhite, and female heads may need food assistance to a greater degree than others, explaining their greater representation among the food stamp user population.

A somewhat different perspective on food stamps and poverty emerges when we examine percentages of families or unrelated individuals *below the poverty line* who did not purchase food stamps in 1974. (See Appendix B, Table B.2.) About 60% of all poor families, and 80% of all poor unrelated individuals did not purchase food stamps in 1974. White, small, and male-headed poor families had relatively low rates of program participation, as did families headed by anyone who was employed.

To summarize, the characteristics of food stamp recipients are somewhat different than those of all poor persons, along lines that would be expected on the basis of location and comparative needs for food assistance. On the other hand, a surprisingly high proportion of all poor persons did not benefit from the program in 1974. Implications for reducing poverty are discussed in what follows, after examining how receiving benefits from other programs affects food stamp households.

MULTIPLE-BENEFIT FOOD STAMP HOUSEHOLDS

Understanding the frequency and type of multiple benefit combinations received by food stamp households allows an informed judgment about two related considerations for federal income transfer policy—income adequacy and work disincentives. In judging the extent to which food stamp households obtain an adequate standard of living, benefits from all sources must be taken into account. The source and levels of those benefits are expected to influence work effort on the part of recipient households, which affects both the overall level of economic activity and the total cost of income-tested federal transfer programs.

Income transfer programs have work disincentive effects because they increase beneficiaries' incomes, thereby enabling them to afford to work less than they might otherwise. Food stamps, as well as other programs, also reduce the gains from work because benefits are reduced for every increment in earnings. Moreover, when the earned income of households receiving benefits from more than one program increases, the rates of benefit reduction cumulate, strengthening the disincentive (see Hausman, 1975).

Before examining the resources of food stamp households in multiple benefit categories, an especially important effect of food stamp supplementation of Aid to Families with Dependent Children should be explained.

TABLE 5.1

Monthly Value of AFDC Payments, 1973, and Food Stamp Bonus Values, 1974, Four-Person Family with No Earned Income, Selected States

State	Maximum AFDC payment[a]	Food stamp bonus value[b]	Total family resources
Five states with lowest maximum payment for basic needs			
Alabama	$104	$117	$221
Arkansas	130	111	241
Louisiana	110	114	224
Mississippi	60	142	202
South Carolina	108	120	228
Average[c]	102	121	223
Five states with highest maximum payment for basic needs[d]			
Massachusetts	358	47	405
Michigan	364	53	417
Minnesota	339	53	392
New York	354	47	401
Vermont	335	47	382
Average	350	49	399

Source: Blechman et al. (1974, pp. 178–179).

[a]AFDC payment based on basic needs budget, from U.S. Department of Health, Education, and Welfare, "Public Assistance Programs: Standards for Basic Needs, July 1973."

[b]Assumes that the AFDC Family pays rent at the monthly amount for basic needs under the state's payment standard, using U.S. Department of Agriculture News Release, "Food Stamp Program Expanded" (October 1973).

[c]Unweighted average.

[d]Excludes Alaska and Hawaii.

Food stamps tend to level interstate differentials in transfer payments available to female-headed families with dependent children (see Table 5.1). Because AFDC payments are relatively low in certain states, the food stamp net income of AFDC recipients in those states tends to be lower than those for AFDC cases in high payment states. Consequently, the average amount of bonus stamps received by AFDC households in low payment states exceeds average amount of bonus stamps received in states with more generous AFDC benefits. Hence the state differentials for families obtaining only AFDC benefits are more pronounced than those for families with AFDC and bonus food stamp benefits. Nevertheless, there remain wide variations in resources available to AFDC–food-stamp households among different states.

An examination of data from a November 1973 USDA survey of food stamp recipient households provides the basis for a summary of some other findings about multiple-benefit combinations. (See Appendix B, Tables B.3 and B.4.) The most striking observation is that only 6% of all food stamp households receive only food stamp benefits. Among the benefit combinations observed, the relatively frequent categories included food stamps and Social Security, Medicare, Aid to Families with Dependent Children, or School Lunch. Far less frequent combinations included general assistance (that is, local relief), Veterans' Benefits, or Unemployment Compensation. On the whole, households received public benefits per person that were roughly twice the amount of income per person from private sources (for example, earnings of household members, or contributions from relatives). And as expected, a ranking of combinations by average public benefits per person revealed that the greater the number of programs assisting a household, the greater the average benefit per person.

Because income levels do not necessarily reflect income adequacy because household needs differ, the adequacy of total incomes (public and private) received on average by households in various multiple benefit categories was assessed with respect to the Community Services Administration's 1973 poverty income threshold guidelines. Although juxtaposing average total incomes with poverty standards tells us little about the actual frequency of inadequate incomes, these comparisons do suggest which groups are likely to have a concentration of households with inadequate incomes. By this standard, food stamp recipients who received either no other benefits or only School Lunch appeared to have the least adequate incomes. In addition, combined benefits apparently fail to remove many Social-Security–food-stamp recipients from poverty, since their average incomes fail to exceed the nonfarm poverty guidelines. Only the relatively infrequent Unemployment Compensation and Veterans' Benefits categories displayed average incomes exceeding the poverty standards. Thus there are substantial disparities in income adequacy for food stamp households, associated with particular benefit combinations. Whether or not one deems these differences large and of serious concern for welfare policy will depend on tastes for income redistribution as well as concern for other factors, particularly the ethic that prescribes work instead of welfare.

To provide a rudimentary assessment of the work disincentives associated with eligibility for food stamps, we estimated the increment to household income attributable to bonus food stamps for important multiple benefit categories, using the June 1973 Current Population Survey tape. The relevant comparisons of total (cash plus food stamp) income for eligible households (cash income below 125% of the poverty line) that did and did not receive food stamps in May 1973 are presented in Appendix B, Tables B.5 and B.6. The general assistance category was found to exhibit the largest increment in income attributable to food stamps. In this category, the average addition of $600 in food stamp benefits to combined general assistance payments and earned income is sufficient to offset the greater earned incomes of general assistance recipients who did not obtain food stamps. Possibly, the availability of food stamps may have encouraged a reduction in labor supply among these recipients. In the context of the Food Stamp program, it is this possibility that best illustrates the tradeoff between providing adequate incomes and maintaining work incentives. Nevertheless, it is important to note that empirical evidence from the New Jersey Negative Income Tax Experiment (Symposium, 1974) suggests that transfer payments need not cause substantial reductions in work effort. William A. Morrill (1974) summarizes the experiment's findings:

> They clearly indicate that a negative tax type plan with a basic benefit as high as the official poverty line will not trigger large-scale reductions in work effort among male heads of families. Indeed, there is no evidence here that even a small proportion of male heads would drop out of the labor-force completely in response to such a plan; small labor-supply reductions are likely to be evenly spread over large numbers of workers. Without a mandatory work requirement, the male heads of families maintained high levels of labor-force participation under all of the experimental plans [p. 157].

In summary, when households receive food stamps in combination with benefits from other programs, their incomes increase. Because food stamp benefits decline as other income increases, households that are also assisted by less generous cash transfers tend to gain relatively more from the stamps (for example, general assistance recipients, or AFDC recipients residing in the South). By contrast, recipients of benefits from social insurance or pension programs (Unemployment Insurance, Veterans' Benefits, Social Security) receive small food stamp subsidies. However, these recipients' combined incomes tend to be closer to adequate. Thus food stamp benefits do not entirely close the gap between the incomes of social insurance beneficiaries and those of the welfare population.

POVERTY REDUCTION

According to the official definition of poverty, poor persons are members of households with incomes less than the amount necessary to meet household needs, as estimated for household age–sex composition and farm–nonfarm residence. Operationally, the Census Bureau counts poor persons on the basis of total household income, which includes the cash income of all household members before taxes and after cash transfer payments. However, because in-kind income adds to household resources, most economists agree that it should also be included in total household income for purposes of comparison with household need standards. In this view, the failure to count in-kind income implies that many officially poor persons should be counted among the nonpoor.

This section summarizes the findings of studies intended to determine how many prestamp poor persons are counted among the nonpoor when bonus food stamps are added to total household income. Included in this description is evidence about target efficiency, as measured by the percentage of all food stamp recipients who were poor according to the official prestamp poverty definition. Of course, this measure is indicative of the program's poverty reduction effect, because the program cannot reduce poverty if it does not reach the poor.

Two studies provide evidence about the program's poverty reduction effect, assuming food stamps are effectively cash. In other words, these studies assume that recipients value their bonus stamps at face value. This simplifying assumption means that we count every bonus stamp dollar as a dollar in cash, although estimates of cash equivalent values from Chapter 3 do suggest that this assumption will introduce some error when applied to small and very poor households.

In order to determine whether a household receiving food stamps is removed from poverty by the additional income from stamps, three things must be known—the household's income without bonus food stamps (prestamp income), the household's income including bonus stamps (poststamp income), and the poverty income threshold for that household. Using data from the Bureau of the Census Current Population Surveys of March and April 1975, Coder (1975) estimated the impact of food stamps on incomes and poverty status for the nation in 1974. Table 5.2 presents Coder's findings. For all persons who purchased food stamps in 1974, the addition of stamp bonuses to prestamp income reduced the percentage below the low-income (poverty) line from 55 to 46%. Expressed as a percentage of prestamp poor recipients, this amounts to a 16% poverty

TABLE 5.2
Families and Persons with Income below the Low Income Level in 1974 before and after
Addition of Annual Food Stamp Bonus Values

	With income below the low income level before addition of bonus		With income below the low income level after addition of bonus	
	Number (thousands)	Percentage	Number (thousands)	Percentage
Total				
Total persons	24,260	11.6	22,714	10.9
In families	19,440	10.2	17,973	9.4
Unrelated Individuals	4,820	25.5	4,741	25.1
Total families	5,109	9.2	4,748	8.5
Purchased food stamps in 1974				
Total persons	9,427	55.2	7,881	46.1
In families	8,715	54.0	7,248	45.0
Unrelated Individuals	712	74.6	633	66.3
Total families	2,064	52.6	1,703	43.4
Purchased food stamps 12 months of 1974				
Total persons	5,863	70.6	4,643	55.9
In families	5,412	69.8	4,260	54.9
Unrelated Individuals	451	82.2	383	69.7
Total families	1,255	67.1	974	52.1

Source: Coder (1975, Table 3).

reduction rate. Among persons who purchased food stamps in all 12 months of 1974, the poverty reduction rate was substantially higher— 21%. Across the entire poverty population (24.3 million persons in 1974), Coder estimated that the poverty reduction rate was only 6.4%.

Coder's estimate that the additions of bonus stamp income to pre-stamp income reduces the official poverty count by 6% in 1974 should be taken as a lower-bound figure for the program's poverty reduction effect, for two reasons. First, he reports that the Current Population Survey undercounts recipients by 19% of the official Department of Agriculture total for July 1974. Second, his estimated bonus value received by families and unrelated individuals participating in the program in 1974 was $2.6 billion, 74% of the USDA figure for 1974. Janis Peskin (1976) estimates that the poverty reduction rate across the entire population would have been about 8% if persons who did not report using food stamps were removed from poverty at the same rate as those who did report using stamps.

In another study MacDonald (1975a) estimated poverty reduction rates for each state. When these estimates are aggregated to produce an estimate for the nation as a whole, we find a substantially greater poverty reduction rate than Coder—16%. Peskin compared MacDonald's estimates to Coder's, concluding that the former "estimates are biased upward by the methodologies utilized in the estimates [p. 57]." It is our opinion that Peskin's interpretation of the Coder study underestimates the program's effects, because she did not correct for *underreporting* of bonus stamps on the part of persons who *did* report the use of food stamps in 1974. It seems safe to conclude that the true national food stamp poverty reduction rate is above 8%, but probably below 16%. The availability of a new Current Population Survey (the Survey of Income and Education) should permit more precise estimation.

In our study, rough, but indicative, estimates of poverty reduction effects by state were derived from 1970 Census and March–April 1975 Current Population Survey data. In short, the method of estimation was to apply 1974 national data on the prestamp income distribution and average food stamp incomes of recipient households to 1974 state participant totals and to total state food stamp incomes. Insofar as either a state's actual participant income distribution or state average food stamp income deviates from corresponding national values, this method is crude. However, an adjustment of national average food stamp incomes before application to states does correct for systematic differences among states in food stamp income levels. The method also accounts for differences among state income distributions, because 1974 state food stamp participant distributions were projected on the basis of actual 1969 state household income distributions. Nevertheless, the results of the analysis are best viewed as "ballpark" estimates of the food stamp program's poverty reduction effect.

Table 5.3 provides percentage estimates of the food stamp program's poverty reduction effect, as well as related measures that indicate how this effect works. The range in the percentage reduction of prestamp poverty among states is striking. Ignoring Alaska, Hawaii, and the District of Columbia, the percentage by which food stamps reduce poverty ranges from .3% in New Hampshire to over 32% in New Jersey. It is also instruc-

TABLE 5.3

Summary Measures of the Food Stamp Poverty Reduction Effect, for States in 1974

	Prestamp poor food stamp recipients as a percentage of the total prestamp poverty population	Prestamp poor food stamp recipients as a percentage of all food stamp recipients	Poststamp nonpoor food stamp recipients as a percentage of prestamp poor food stamp recipients	Poststamp nonpoor food stamp recipients as a percentage of the total prestamp poverty population
Alabama	26.9	62.8	32.9	8.8
Alaska	37.3	54.7	74.0	27.6
Arizona	23.8	55.9	28.3	6.7
Arkansas	32.8	61.8	44.5	14.6
California	40.4	51.8	50.5	20.4
Colorado	28.9	52.3	41.7	10.9
Connecticutt	46.8	48.9	52.4	24.5
Delaware	16.0	48.9	24.5	3.9
D.C.	76.5	58.2	84.0	64.2
Florida	26.6	53.2	40.9	10.9
Georgia	29.8	61.4	30.3	9.0
Hawaii	64.9	49.3	86.2	55.9
Idaho	18.7	5.0	27.1	5.1
Illinois	44.1	52.9	67.3	29.6
Indiana	21.8	45.2	27.9	6.1
Iowa	19.7	47.1	28.5	5.6
Kansas	9.2	50.0	7.9	0.7
Kentucky	46.4	63.5	57.2	26.5
Louisiana	40.4	67.1	56.9	23.0
Maine	30.0	46.4	55.7	16.7
Maryland	44.8	51.9	69.4	31.1
Massachusetts	9.4	47.7	20.2	1.9

Michigan	31.3	33.4	46.2	25.0
Minnesota	24.7	49.7	31.0	7.7
Mississippi	36.7	70.9	39.2	14.4
Missouri	24.7	53.7	32.5	8.0
Montana	21.1	50.8	31.1	6.6
Nebraska	13.9	52.9	14.6	2.0
Nevada	24.6	37.0	39.3	9.7
New Hampshire	11.5	45.7	2.2	0.3
New Jersey	48.8	46.6	66.6	32.5
New Mexico	45.8	61.9	64.7	29.6
New York	39.0	50.4	37.7	14.7
North Carolina	22.6	57.1	23.5	5.3
North Dakota	12.5	52.5	7.2	0.9
Ohio	46.6	51.4	67.4	31.4
Oklahoma	18.0	52.9	19.9	3.6
Oregon	39.2	50.9	53.9	21.1
Pennsylvania	38.7	46.8	46.6	18.0
Rhode Island	50.1	53.9	52.2	26.1
South Carolina	43.2	60.8	60.2	26.0
South Dakota	14.8	51.7	11.7	1.7
Tennessee	30.5	57.9	38.0	11.6
Texas	36.3	56.3	51.6	18.7
Utah	22.2	52.7	16.7	3.7
Vermont	47.2	49.6	50.9	24.0
Virginia	19.6	54.6	19.9	3.9
Washington	45.1	48.9	70.5	31.8
West Virginia	14.1	60.5	43.8	6.2
Wisconsin	18.5	49.8	14.0	2.6
Wyoming	13.4	51.6	18.0	2.4
U.S. Total	*34.1*	*54.3*	*47.7*	*16.3*

tive to note that Mountain West and Midwest states predominate among states with very low poverty reduction effects. Correspondingly, Table 5.3 indicates these states have relatively low percentages of poor persons receiving food stamps. The policy implication is that increasing participation would substantially reduce poverty in the nation's heartland.

This same conclusion can be extended to the entire nation, since only 34% of all poor persons received food stamps in 1974. (This figure, taken from Table 5.3, is roughly comparable to the 39% figure that can be derived from Coder's results in Table 5.2.) Beyond this, caution should be exercised in interpreting Table 5.3. Using August 1974 Current Population Survey data on 12 heavily populated states, Peskin (1976) found that the ranking of state poverty reduction effects differed considerably from our results. These differences stem from a variety of sources, including differential sampling error, errors introduced by the assumptions used to generate state income distributions for our analysis, and differences between the actual population of stamp recipients in Peskin's August 1974 sample and the "average annual" figures used in our study. These differences are associated with month to month turnover in the recipient population, which is ignored to some extent in our attempt to obtain estimates for an annual period.

The results of this section have implications for attempts to achieve two federal welfare policy goals: the efficient allocation of funds for social investment (for example, educational expenditure); and the reduction of poverty.

Congress frequently allocates federal funds for state-administered social programs on the basis of relative need, as measured in part by the relative size of state poverty populations. If, as our findings suggest, official measures of state poverty are deficient, the current allocation of federal funds is inefficient. Thus one policy conclusion from this study is that data on food stamp income should be gathered by existing Census instruments for inclusion in the official poverty measures. In addition, other in-kind benefits ought to be incorporated in those measures, assuming those benefits would also affect the relative size of state poverty counts.

With respect to the related goal of reducing poverty, an inference from Table 5.3 is that increasing the rate of Food Stamp program participation among the prestamp poor would greatly reduce the number of poststamp poor. Because many states have relatively small food stamp poverty reduction effects, it follows that substantial progress toward eliminating poverty could result from efforts to promote food stamp use. The next chapter suggests how program participation might be increased.

SUMMARY

Although the majority of food stamp recipients are prestamp poor, food stamps augment other transfer payments available to both nonpoor and poor households. Because a household's food stamp income is inversely related to its combined income from all other sources, the program's major role in the income-maintenance system is to reduce income inequality among system beneficiaries. Food stamps narrow the interstate differentials in the total resources of welfare mothers, they reduce the gap in the average prestamp incomes of AFDC and General Assistance recipients, and they offer the only source of income support to low-income persons failing to qualify for categorical assistance programs. An undesirable side effect of the Food Stamp Program's contribution to low incomes is that work disincentives are increased. Incentives to work are further reduced by the cumulation of benefit loss rates on earned income for multiple benefit households. However, evidence from a Negative Income Tax experiment suggests that income transfer programs do not drastically affect labor supply.

By the standard of the official poverty line, food stamp incomes are not large enough to provide adequate incomes for all recipients. Moreover, considerably less than half of all officially poor persons obtained stamps during 1974. On the other hand, food stamps were found to reduce the official poverty count by over 8% in 1974. Since the program cannot reduce poverty unless it enrolls poor eligibles, attacking poverty would seem to require greater enrollment.

In conclusion, the food stamp program plays an important role in supplementing the incomes of working and nonworking poor families, but that role could be expanded.

6

Participation in the
Food Stamp Program

Since 1968, the Food Stamp program has been criticized for its inability to enroll even a majority of those eligible. Because eligibility is primarily restricted to households whose financial resources indicate they cannot purchase a minimally adequate diet without food stamps, the welfare implication of this criticism is quite serious. As the Food Stamp program is the only universally available income-support program bridging the gap between welfare recipients and low-income working families, the program has also been criticized for not reaching members of the "working poor."

There is empirical support for these criticisms. According to estimates prepared by the Office of Income Security Policy and Analysis of the Department of Health, Education, and Welfare, the number of persons eligible for food stamps on the basis of annual income projections for 1974 was approximately 37 million, whereas the number of food stamp participants over the first three quarters of 1974 averaged less than 13.7 million. Thus well under 40% of all persons entitled to obtain food stamps actually received them in 1974. However, at that time, food stamp enrollment was on the rise, due to geographic expansion of the program combined with increasing need for income supplementation on the part of households that were adversely affected by the recession. Thus the food stamp participation rate has undoubtedly increased somewhat since 1974. Still, a preliminary estimate is that less than half of all eligibles received stamps in 1976.[1]

The intent of this chapter is to examine empirically the problem of low food stamp participation and to recommend remedial policies. If progress toward more adequate food stamp participation is to be monitored, information on participation rates at the state level is necessary, owing to the states' responsibility for overseeing food stamp operations at the local level. Thus, estimates of participation rates for each state are presented, and the pattern of participation across states is discussed. Then the issue of whether or not eligible nonparticipants are disproportionately composed of relatively well-off families is addressed, using national survey data. Those survey data also provide an opportunity for a multivariate study of household characteristics associated with low probabilities of food stamp use. Tentative conclusions for food stamp policy are expressed and then summarized.

PARTICIPATION RATES AND NEED

Federal regulations specify uniform national standards for the maximum levels of income and assets that a household of a particular size may have and still qualify for food stamps. The income standard is the more fundamental determinant of eligibility. Bickel and MacDonald (1975) obtained estimates of the number of persons with 1974 incomes lower than the income standard for food stamp eligibility. For each state and size of household, the data requirements for these estimates were (a) a cumulative percentage distribution of households by income, (b) the Food Stamp program's maximum allowable income, and (c) the total number of households. By applying the appropriate income maximum to each cumulative percentage distribution, the percentage of all households of a given size eligible for food stamps was estimated.

Next, multiplication of the resulting percentage by the number of

---

[1]During calender 1976, the peak number of monthly stamp recipients was less than half of the eligible population estimated for 1974. Assuming some growth in the eligible population from 1974 to 1976 therefore implies a 1976 participation rate of less than 50%.

households of that size produced the estimated number of eligible house-holds. These two steps were repeated for each household size. Then, multiplying the number of eligible households by their respective sizes and cumulating products gave the total number of eligible persons in the state.

This procedure would have been quite simple had the necessary data been available in the proper form. Instead, existing decennial census data for 1969 were used to generate state income distributions appropriate for 1974, based on the assumption that the ratio of state to national percent-ages of households below each income-class boundary remained constant. This assumption produced fewer eligible households in 1974 than in 1969, while maintaining the 1969 ranking of states by the proportion of house-holds below the food stamp program's net income maximum.

In addition to generating state household income distributions, there were a number of other important complications for estimating 1974 state eligible populations. Preliminary total numbers of eligible persons in each state were revised to reflect the net effect of the following considerations:

1. There was an allowance for overcount because some households eligible on income grounds have assets too large to allow them to qualify.
2. Because the household income data are limited to total money income, the preliminary totals based on those data failed to include many persons whose net income after allowable deductions made them eligible. In adjusting for this divergence between household total money income and food stamp net income, the fact that the Current Population Survey data underreports household total money income was also taken into account.
3. During 1974, all recipients of Supplemental Security Income in California, Massachusetts, Wisconsin, New York, and Nevada were categorically ineligible for food stamps, requiring a special downward adjustment in the estimates for these states.
4. Because normal household income fluctuates during any year, the use of annual income data in determining eligibility for a program that operates on a monthly income basis produces a significant net undercount of the true size of the eligible population. Existing estimates of the degree of income variability both within and be-tween calendar-year periods provided an appropriate correction factor.

The resulting final estimates of the number of persons eligible are presented in Column 1 of Table 6.1, for each state and for the entire

TABLE 6.1
State Food Stamp Participation Rates

State	Estimated number of persons eligible in 1974 (1)	Peak monthly number of participants Jan. – Sept. 1974 (2)	Estimated 1974 participation rate (3) = (2) ÷ (1)
Alabama	1,177,139	338,762	28.8
Alaska	71,968	21,769	30.2
Arizona	421,552	111,520	26.5
Arkansas	754,353	249,514	33.0
California	2,412,481	1,404,824	58.2
Colorado	411,554	138,567	33.6
Connecticut	291,513	145,313	49.8
Delaware	85,458	21,214	24.8
D.C.	150,783	117,830	78.1
Florida	1,713,309	514,847	30.0
Georgia	1,318,000	424,830	32.2
Hawaii	160,839	71,540	44.5
Idaho	161,812	33,794	20.9
Illinois	1,569,158	878,455	56.0
Indiana	771,298	194,791	25.5
Iowa	510,030	116,020	22.7
Kansas	425,533	53,107	12.5
Kentucky	1,053,952	401,992	38.1
Louisiana	1,269,096	530,589	41.8
Maine	212,394	96,133	45.3
Maryland	560,352	258,710	46.2
Massachusetts	612,749	284,966	46.5
Michigan	1,156,822	581,754	50.3
Minnesota	599,682	184,142	30.7
Mississippi	982,632	351,117	35.4
Missouri	1,074,852	290,932	27.1
Montana	147,786	33,393	22.2
Nebraska	299,628	50,447	16.8
Nevada	65,924	27,168	41.2
New Hampshire	102,000	32,000	31.3
New Jersey	833,394	435,187	52.2
New Mexico	351,627	149,831	42.6
New York	2,447,536	1,195,785	48.9
North Carolina	1,484,562	341,397	23.0
North Dakota	155,072	18,361	11.8
Ohio	1,517,172	750,774	49.5
Oklahoma	691,202	155,463	22.5
Oregon	346,542	163,617	47.2

TABLE 6.1 *(Continued)*

State	Estimated number of persons eligible in 1974 (1)	Peak monthly number of participants Jan. – Sept. 1974 (2)	Estimated 1974 participation rate (3) = (2) ÷ (1)
Pennsylvania	1,814,010	744,896	41.1
Rhode Island	143,388	77,881	54.3
South Carolina	859,161	354,484	41.3
South Dakota	204,789	30,273	14.8
Tennessee	1,247,504	329,456	26.4
Texas	3,007,732	1,057,976	35.2
Utah	188,742	39,829	21.1
Vermont	82,382	38,165	46.3
Virginia	1,030,544	215,338	20.9
Washington	475,084	228,898	48.2
West Virginia	543,888	213,774	39.3
Wisconsin	609,985	129,403	21.2
Wyoming	62,325	9,272	14.9
Total U.S.	*38,623,810*	*14,411,501*	*37.5*

Source: Bickel and MacDonald (1975).

nation. Column 2 displays the peak number of food stamp participants through September 1974. Division of the Column 2 figures by the corresponding Column 1 figures produces the percentages of eligibles using food stamps, shown in Column 3. Summing all of the table's estimates of state eligible populations, we obtain 38.6 million persons as a conservative estimate of the number eligible in the nation in 1974. This national figure compares favorably the HEW estimate of 37 million and implies a 1974 food stamp program participation rate below 40%.

Looking at the rates for individual states reveals striking differences in participation levels, ranging from 14.9% in Wyoming to 55.7% in California. The 10 states with the lowest participation rates all have less than 22% participation, whereas each of the 10 states with the highest rates, has more than 45% participation. With the exception of Alaska and Virginia, the 10 lowest-participation states are located in the heartland: Idaho, Iowa, Kansas, North Dakota, Nebraska, Utah, Wisconsin, and Wyoming. By contrast, either coastal location or more highly populated and industrial structure characterize the 10 highest-participation states—California, Connecticut, Illinois, Michigan, New Jersey, New York, Ohio, Oregon, Rhode Island, and Washington. Again excepting Virginia, all of the southern states rank among the middle 30 with Louisiana, Kentucky, and South Carolina displaying above-average participation rates.

Although differences in attitudes toward government assistance on the part of both eligible households and taxpayers certainly provide an appealing explanation for the divergence among states in food stamp participation, in many instances states with quite similar economic and social structures differ in food stamp usage. Examples can be found in every major region. Wisconsin ranks in the bottom 10, whereas Michigan and Illinois are in the top 10. Nevada's rate of participation substantially exceeds that of neighboring Idaho. Virginia and Delaware are also distinguished in their regions by relatively low participation.

Whatever the sources of these variations in state food stamp participation, evidently they also operate at the local level. For example, the counties along Wisconsin's northern border have very similar geography and economy but markedly different participation rates. Surprisingly, there is even substantial variation across Wisconsin Standard Metropolitan Statistical Areas, ranging from a low of around 25% in Madison to 40% in Milwaukee and over 45% in Superior (MacDonald, 1975b). In a study of participation in Minnesota's food stamp program, Sexauer et al. (1976) found similar variations among geographic areas. Because we expect a more uniform response to the availability of food stamps among counties with highly similar eligible populations, these variations would appear to stem, at least in part, from the administrative practices of county food stamp agencies, since potential food stamp recipients must deal with the officials and authorized representatives of local food stamp agencies, who can encourage or discourage participation by the extent to which they conduct food stamp transactions with convenience and respect for recipients.

An argument against emphasizing what might be termed the supply side of the market for food stamps is that those eligibles really in need of assistance will take whatever steps are necessary to get it. From this standpoint, observed differences in county and state participation rates simply result from the distribution of needy eligibles among political subunits, and the fact that the nation's participation rate was less than 40% in 1974 merely implies that only this percentage of eligibles really needed government food aid. Many of the persons eligible for food stamps qualify for relatively small bonus amounts, especially when measured against the costs of getting and using them. Therefore, there must be a sizable group of eligible nonparticipants that chooses not to enroll in the program.

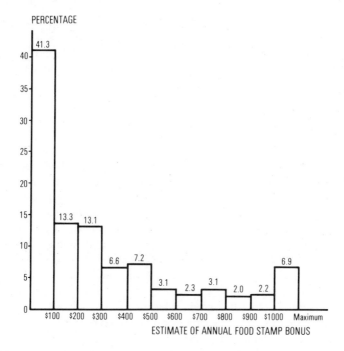

Figure 6.1. *Percentage distribution of eligible nonparticipant households by 1971 annual food stamp bonus estimate.*

Because the food stamp benefit schedule allocates greater benefits to needier households, it is possible to test this argument by examining a sample of eligible households for which benefit amounts have been calculated. A finding that a sizable proportion of the food stamp eligible population fails to collect bonus amounts that would substantially increase their purchasing power would certainly deserve attention as evidence that food stamp participation levels are "too low." Figure 6.1 presents this evidence. For a representative national sample of households from the 1972 interview wave of the Michigan Panel Study of Income Dynamics (Morgan *et al.,* 1972) the figure displays a percentage distribution of eligible nonparticipants according to estimates of the size of the annual food stamp bonus for which they were eligible in 1971.[2] As expected, the graph shows that a

<hr>

[2]As explained in Footnote 3, the Michigan Panel data do provide a reasonable approximation of household net income under food stamp regulations. Using these net income measures and the program's benefit schedule, an eligibility determination and an annualized food stamp bonus are readily obtained for each sample household.

high proportion of nonparticipants would receive relatively small food stamp bonus amounts. Yet about one-third of the nonparticipants were eligible for, but did not get, bonus food stamps worth more than $300 per year. And over 10% were eligible for, but did not collect, bonus stamps worth $800 or more.

EXPLAINING NONPARTICIPATION

Perhaps the most obvious potential reason that persons eligible for sizable benefits do not enroll is ignorance, either about the existence of food stamps or about the amount of benefits to which their household is entitled. Congress foresaw the possibility that eligibles might not learn of the program and provided a mechanism to overcome this difficulty. The Food Stamp Act of 1964 established a formula for matching federal funds with state funds for conducting outreach activities to inform eligibles about the food stamp program. Moreover, the act stipulated the responsibility of the USDA to require state food stamp agencies to do outreach or risk losing those federal dollars that support bonus stamp payments. Nevertheless, in 1974 a Minnesota U.S. District Court ordered the USDA to develop and implement an effective outreach campaign. Based on evidence presented by the plaintiffs in *Bennett* v. *Butz,* a class-action suit on behalf of welfare rights advocates, Judge Miles Lord found that Minnesota and the USDA had never conducted outreach in the manner prescribed by federal law. Thus there is reason to believe that some poor persons are uninformed about food stamps.

Barring ignorance, eligibles will choose not to participate when program benefits are less than the costs of participation. An eligible household's preferences for food versus other goods dictates the cash equivalent value of bonus stamps available to the household. Since the household must pay a purchase price to get that cash equivalent value, it sacrifices some other goods to obtain program benefits. Thus the purchase price of the stamp allotment is one important component of the full cost of program participation. In addition, there are user costs associated with participation. These user costs include the costs of getting and spending food stamps, to which no monetary value can be attached. These costs can be divided into access costs and stigma costs.

Access costs include all the time and trouble it takes to get certified for, to purchase, and to use food stamps. Applying for food stamps can be very inconvenient, especially if there is a long wait to see a caseworker or if a return visit is required to provide a receipt or verification that all employable household members are work-registered.

Perhaps intangible stigma costs also discourage food stamp participation. According to Weisbrod (1970), those costs are associated with the loss of self-respect, dignity, and acceptance by the rest of society that occurs when persons make their poverty known to others in order to receive benefits from a transfer program. In the course of handling and using food stamps, there is ample opportunity for recipients to suffer these stigma costs. Besides having to fully inform a caseworker about one's finances at a welfare office to gain authorization to purchase the stamps, many food stamp users must see an employment officer or buy stamps from a bank clerk or a postal service employee. Then, once in hand, the stamps must be spent in public.

Both kinds of user costs probably vary in importance, depending on the circumstances of the potential user. For instance, persons raised in families that castigated welfare recipients are more likely to resist taking food stamps for reasons of stigma avoidance than are second-generation welfare recipients. Other examples of factors causing differential user costs easily come to mind, such as the degree to which the potential recipient's free time coincides with the hours that food stamp offices are open, whether or not babysitting arrangements are necessary, and, for the aged and disabled, physical ability to travel to a food stamp agency may be important.

Although there are rudimentary surveys that ask about reasons for nonparticipation (Rungeling and Smith, 1975), no survey has yet been designed specifically to capture variations in stigma and access costs and to measure eligible households' knowledge of the Food Stamp Program. An ideal analysis of food stamp participation would require such a survey, as well as variables reflecting the degree to which local food stamp agencies facilitate or obstruct enrollment of legitimate eligibles. Without minimizing the fact that this unique combination of data is unavailable, it is possible to report results from a study based on a reasonably good substitute.

The 1972 interview wave of the Panel Study of Income Dynamics asked respondents from its 5000-household representative national sample whether they had used food stamps at any time during 1971. In addition, the 1972 interview collected detailed information about the 1971 income of the household and about many other socioeconomic and demographic characteristics. Using these characteristics, we first isolated a subset of households, living in counties with food stamp projects, whose 1971 estimated net income levels (after allowable deductions) or status as a public assistance recipient indicated they were eligible for food stamps that year.[3] All eligibles were then divided into two groups—participants and nonparticipants. Variables constructed from other household data were then used to predict which eligibles actually used food stamps in 1971.[4]

Before summarizing how the various predictors are related to levels of food stamp participation, let us discuss the rationale for selecting these predictors. From information about the sources and uses of annual household income, a net income measure reasonably approximating annual food stamp net income was constructed. Using this measure and an annualized food stamp benefit schedule, it was possible to estimate the food stamp bonus each household would receive if it participated for the entire year 1971. For households with stable incomes, this measure correctly reflects the annual level of benefits a household can expect from food stamps. However, if incomes fluctuate markedly during the year, bonus amounts calculated from annual net income may not reflect the true sum of available monthly food stamp benefits. To account for such fluctuations, we hold constant the number of hours the household head was underemployed in 1971. As defined for our purposes, "hours underemployed" refers to that portion of a 2000 hour "work year" that the head did not spend on the job. Thus persons not in the labor force and fully employed persons both have zero underemployment hours. For this reason, it was also necessary to include a variable for whether or not the head was in the labor force during 1971, as well as the variable based on hours worked.

To a large extent, the bonus amount indicates the degree of household need for food stamps. If that need is temporary, however, eligibles may rely on their savings or simply cut down on expenses until their income returns to some normally higher level, especially if stigma is an important component of user costs. By including the household's reserve fund position and an index of decile position in the household income—

---

[3] As explained in Chapter 2, the food stamp net income definition is quite complicated. A host of deductions are subtracted from total household income (see page 25 for a full listing). The Michigan Panel data allow a conservative estimate of household net income. Only federal income taxes, union dues, and child care expenses were subtracted from total family income to estimate net income.

[4] Multiple discriminant analysis and classification procedures provided the multivariate technique for isolating a set of variables in one random split-half of the eligible sample that classified 70% of the remaining holdout split-half sample into the correct participant or

needs distribution (based on a 4-year average, defined with respect to the cost of purchasing a low-cost diet for all household members), any divergence of 1971 needs from those of the recent past is effectively controlled. In part, the reserve fund variable may also reflect the assets test for program eligibility, since our procedure for determining eligibility is fairly crude with respect to assets.

Most of the remaining predictors can be viewed as indicators of knowledge about the program or of differential user costs. City size and census region enter the predictive model for both purposes. Survey respondents in the largest-city category, but none of those in areas with cities of less than 10,000, reported access to good public transportation. The degree to which information about food stamps is disseminated probably also varies by city size. And perhaps food stamp agencies publicize the program to a greater extent in certain census regions.

A household's receptivity to information about food stamps probably depends on specific attributes, perhaps including some measured by the status of the household head with regard to education, sentence completion test score, student or nonstudent status; and some measured by a household index of connections to potential sources of information, based on items like attendance at church or union meetings, visits to taverns, and acquaintance with neighbors.

Age of the household head might also capture differences in receptivity to information, but it could also capture varying stigma costs as well. One hypothesis is that unfavorable attitudes toward receiving government assistance have been diminishing and, therefore, older people are more likely to maintain feelings about stigma that are gradually becoming outmoded. Another stigma hypothesis is that people are less likely to feel stigmatized when similarly situated persons are also needy. This implies less sensitivity to stigma in depressed areas, which are indicated by the unemployment rate for the household's county of residence.

Finally, welfare recipients are often certified for food stamp eligibility when they apply for welfare payments. Consequently households receiving welfare either during or prior to 1971 should be more likely to use food stamps. In addition to knowing more about the program, welfare recipients have demonstrated their ability to overcome the user costs associated with welfare, which presumably are comparable in magnitude to the user costs of food stamps.

---

nonparticipant category. Among the variables that did not add to the predictive power of this analysis were sex and race of the household head.

Results

Our results are best understood when presented in a multiple regression format known as multiple classification analysis.[5] Table 6.2 presents the multiple regression of household characteristics on a dichotomous dependent variable for whether or not the household used food stamps in 1971.[6] The regressors shown in the table are categories of each independent variable. For each of these categories, the table presents the percentage of all sample households that used food stamps in 1971, to indicate the bivariate relationship of each predictor to food stamp usage. Alongside those percentages are category adjusted means, which are the multiple regression-predicted percentage of food stamp users within each category, holding constant the influence of all other categories. By examining these adjusted means, one can determine the net effect of a given independent variable on the likelihood of food stamp participation. Tests of statistical significance revealed that only three of the regression coefficients estimated for our predictor categories were not statistically different from zero.

The results do yield support for our reasoning about participation of welfare recipients. The predicted percentage of food stamp users (53%) among welfare recipients is about twice that among households without welfare income (27%). Coupled with the result that households headed by persons not in the labor force are also more likely to use food stamps than households with employable heads, this finding suggests that one important source of low food stamp participation rates is that the program fails to enroll eligibles who have attachments to the labor force and no welfare

---

[5]Multiple classification analysis (MCA) is dummy variable regression with all independent variables in dummy (categorical) form. However, MCA differs from standard dummy variable regression in that it uses a constant auxiliary to that employed in minimizing squared errors, to produce coefficients for every category of all predictors. These coefficients are deviations from the grand mean of the dependent variable, owing to category membership, when deviations due to all other predictor categories are taken into account. Thus the predicted values for the dependent variable within each category are equal to the grand mean plus the MCA coefficient for the category. See Melichar (1966).

[6]As indicated in Footnote 4, we also performed a multiple discriminant analysis of food stamp participation. Discriminant analysis avoids the statistical problems associated with multiple regression analysis of a dichotomous dependent variable. For all practical purposes, the results of our discriminant analysis are identical to the multiple regression results presented in Table 6.2. Thus, it is safe to conclude that the results in Table 6.2 are valid, despite our use of a dichotomous dependent variable. We chose to present Table 6.2 to facilitate understanding on the part of laypersons.

income. A policy implication is that increasing food stamp participation rates will require an effort targeted at "working poor."

In support of our multivariate approach, note that the pattern of actual participation by food stamp bonus category is quite the opposite of that predicted when other influences are held constant. Most participants belong to the group entitled to bonus amounts worth $200 or less. A separate cross tabulation revealed that this anomaly is explained by the relatively high net incomes of some welfare recipients (implying low annual bonuses) who still tend to use food stamps, probably as a result of their relatively low user costs.

We also find substantial evidence that participation does increase with the household's need for assistance, as determined by the patterns of adjusted means for the annual food stamp bonus, the household reserve fund position, and the 4-year score on decile position in the income−needs ranking. The differentials in predicted participation rates are substantial, ranging from 34 to 61% across food stamp bonus categories.

Predicted program participation rates for most categories of the connectedness index—the head's sentence completion score, the head's education, and whether the head is a student—are quite similar to the actual 42% rate of participation for the entire eligible sample of 480 persons. If one accepts these predictors as valid proxies for information about food stamps, it follows that knowledge about the program does not seem to influence participation. On the other hand, it may be that our information indicators simply fail to capture variations in specific knowledge about food stamps.

Returning to Table 6.2, other results can be interpreted to suggest that attempts to change attitudes toward government assistance could contribute to a rise in participation. The patterns of adjusted means for head's age, and especially for the county unemployment rate, are consistent with the hypotheses put forth about the role of stigma. Predicted participation increases uniformly with county unemployment, whereas there is a strong trend toward nonparticipation by households headed by persons over age 65. Of course, neither of these results necessarily implies that stigma is important. Other interpretations are certainly possible.

With respect to explanatory power, only welfare status and the food stamp bonus stood out as powerful predictors net of the other variables, with each explaining roughly 15% of the variance in the dependent variable. Thus relative need may be the most important predictor of participation.

With an important exception, Coe's (1977) analysis of 1973 data

TABLE 6.2

Predictor Category Means from a Multiple Classification Analysis of Food Stamp Participation in 1971

Participation Predictors	Percentage distribution of stamp recipients	Adjusted mean
Population of largest city in PSU		
100,000 or more	.57	.40
25,000–100,000	.15	.42
10,000–25,000	.10	.47[a]
Less than 10,000	.28	.45
Census region		
West	.19	.48
South	.30	.41
North Central	.30	.41
Northeast	.21	.35
Dollar amount of 1971 food stamp bonus		
$200 or less	.45	.34
201–400	.18	.40
401–600	.10	.45
601–800	.06	.44
801–1000	.06	.54
More than $1000	.15	.61
Household reserve fund		
1971 savings exceeding 2 months' income	.20	.18
1971 savings exceeding 2 months' income, but more saved in past 5 years	.07	.39
No 1971 savings, but more than 2 months' income saved in past 5 years	.17	.43
No 1971 savings or less than 2 months' income, and same in past 5 years	.61	.50
Four-year (1968–1971) sum of household decile position in the size distribution of family income-needs ratio		
Less than 10	.81	.44
10 to 20	.16	.36
Greater than 20	.03	.36
Receipt of welfare payments		
Reported welfare income during 1967–1971	.58	.53
No welfare income reported during 1967–1971	.42	.27
Labor force status of head 1971		
In labor force	.40	.35
Not in labor force	.60	.47

TABLE 6.2 (*Continued*)

Participation Predictors	Percentage distribution of stamp recipients	Adjusted mean
Underemployment hours of head in 1971		
Zero	.83	.43
1–500	.04	.34
501–1000	.06	.54
1001–1500	.03	.34
Greater than 1500	.04	.26
County unemployment rate in August 1972		
Under 2%	.02	.27
2.0–3.9%	.16	.31
4.0–5.9%	.44	.42
More than 6.0%	.28	.47
Age of household head		
Less than 25 years	.22	.39
25–44 years	.24	.52
44–65 years	.25	.43
More than 65 years	.29	.35
Index of connectedness to potential sources of help		
0–3	.14	.39
4–5	.41	.45
6–7	.35	.45
8–9	.10	.23
Survey respondent's score on 13-item sentence completion test		
0–3	.06	.46
5–7	.29	.37
8–10	.45	.44[a]
11–13	.20	.42
Education of head		
Finished 0–5 grades	.20	.44
Finished 6–8 grades	.24	.43
Finished 9–11 grades	.26	.39[a]
Finished more than 12 grades	.30	.42
Whether head is student		
Student	.04	.38
Nonstudent	.96	.42

Notes: Adjusted R^2 = .37.
Grand mean = .42.
N = 480.
[a]Indicates the regression coefficient used to adjust the mean was not significant at the .05 level.

from the 1974 Panel Study of Income Dynamics generally supports our findings. Surprisingly, Coe found that participation was not related to the stamp bonus. This conflict among results could be explained by differences in the "average" administrative efficiency of county programs, since many new programs began to operate after 1971; unmeasured factors associated with deteriorating economic conditions in 1974; and differences in sample selection—Coe's sample is restricted to a subsample of eligibles with household income below the poverty line, whereas our 1971 sample includes eligibles with incomes above the poverty line, on the basis of estimated net incomes. At any rate, if Coe's findings are more pertinent than ours, factors other than relative need ought to be emphasized in discussing policies to promote food stamp use.

SUMMARY AND POLICY IMPLICATIONS

This chapter demonstrates there is widespread geographic variability in food stamp participation rates. We also find that a substantial proportion of nonparticipant eligibles will qualify for sizable food stamp bonuses, indicating unmet need. Based on the characteristics of a sample of eligible households from the Michigan Panel Study, we sought to explain in terms of information, access, and stigma costs of program participation why these eligibles fail to use food stamps. Although our multivariate analysis was moderately successful in explaining participation, it is difficult to infer the relative importance of stigma, access, and information costs because some available explanatory variables can be interpreted as indicators of more than one cost. For instance, age of the household head could proxy for both stigma and access costs.

On the other hand, variables that appeared to be useful information indicators were singularly unsuccessful predictors of food stamp use. However, it stands to reason that a household must know of its eligibility to participate—it is difficult to believe that eligible nonparticipants qualifying for sizable bonuses were well informed in 1971. Given this supposition, a policy conclusion is that the Department of Agriculture should strictly enforce its own guidelines for conducting food stamp outreach. In compliance with the uncontested final decision and order in *Bennett v. Butz*, more detailed regulations now govern the procedures for outreach. The regulations define outreach as

> effective, comprehensive ongoing efforts initiated and monitored by the State Agency . . . to inform all low-income households potentially eligible to receive

food stamps of the availability and benefits of the program, and to insure the participation of eligible households that wish to participate by providing such households with reasonable and convenient access to the program [Food Research Action Center 1975, p. 6].

Based on empirical evidence that participation increases with the bonus amount, and the supposition that many eligibles may be uninformed of their eligibility for sizable bonuses, we can predict that effective outreach will specialize in accurately informing eligible households about benefit entitlements. Thus the content of outreach should be governed by the insight that the gains from supplying only general information may be quite limited.

Undoubtedly some nonparticipants choose not to use food stamps because associated access costs exceed expected benefits from participation. Increased efficiency in local food stamp agency operations could contribute to a reduction in food stamp user costs, raising the average net benefit from participation, thereby encouraging greater enrollment in the program. However, if stigma is the most important user cost, policies to reduce access costs may be ill-founded. Although evidence presented here can be interpreted to suggest stigma is important, it is difficult to formulate recommendations for dealing with this barrier to food stamp use. We know very little about how the attitudes that dispose people toward feelings of stigma become ingrained or about how they might change. If stigma arises primarily out of personal perceptions about how one is viewed by others, it may operate less forcefully in some contexts than in others. Thus as more eligibles enroll in the program, stigma could become a minor deterrent, due to a bandwagon effect.

In conclusion, it seems difficult to infer appropriate policies for increasing food stamp participation. Yet the finding that there are substantial numbers of nonparticipants eligible for sizable stamp bonuses would seem to dictate a need for further study. Perhaps experimentation by local program administrators could begin to suggest policies that would induce more eligibles to use stamps.

7

Alternatives for
Food Stamp Reform

The rapid growth in food stamp enrollment after the extension of the program to all counties in the United States and during the 1974–1975 recession subjected program operations to public scrutiny. What that scrutiny revealed alarmed many taxpayers and their representatives. Upon discovering that the program provided benefits to some households with incomes substantially above the official poverty line, Treasury Secretary William Simon (1975) was moved to declare the program "a haven for chiselers and rip-off artists [p. 4]." Presumably, the secretary was concerned about the host of legal allowable deductions that permitted the "chiselers" to receive food stamps. At any rate, there developed a clamor to reform the Food Stamp program. In January 1976, the Ford administration proposed, but could not sustain, a measure that would have reduced food stamp bonuses for some (mostly one- and two-person) recipient households by instituting a uniform purchase price at 30% of household income. Thereafter, other bills intended to cut program benefits and lower the maximum income limits for eligibility were introduced in Congress. Food stamp proponents seemed to welcome the opportunity to reexamine the program's structure, but objected to Secretary Simon's caricature of the program and to the attempts to cut program enrollment. (See Sexauer 1977.) Thus began a lengthy debate on food stamp reform.

In May 1976, the Ford administration proposed to end this debate by unilaterally altering the program through changes in federal regulations, pursuant to the administration's interpretation of the powers granted to the Secretary of Agriculture by the enabling legislation for food stamps. In response, individual plaintiffs, 23 state governments, and numerous organizations filed a request in federal court to prevent the new regulations from taking effect as scheduled for July 1976. As an interim measure, the court granted a temporary injunction to assess the plaintiffs' claims that the proposed regulations were unconstitutional. While the administration's regulations remained in litigation, the House Committee on Agriculture approved its Food Stamp Act of September 1976 (H.R. 13613). In April, the Senate had passed its Food Stamp Reform Act of 1976 (S. 3136).

In the interest of suggesting alternative futures for the Food Stamp Program, this chapter describes the key features of the Ford administration's proposed regulations, the House Committee bill, and the Senate-passed bill. The estimated impact of these bills on various aspects of the program are compared to the existing program, and cost estimates are discussed. Then, two other proposals for reform are examined. One, to eliminate the program's purchase requirement, was originally proposed in Senate reform bill 2451, which was sponsored by Senators Robert Dole and George McGovern (U.S. Senate, 1975). Another is often mentioned in discussions of incremental, or gradual, welfare reform: the replacement of bonus stamps with cash transfers.

THREE AGENDAS FOR REFORM

Table 7.1 summarizes the most important features of the three reform agendas considered in this section, and compares them to existing program regulations.

Purchase Requirements

Under the present Food Stamp program, most beneficiary households are required to pay about 30% of their net income (income after allowable deductions) for food stamps. Given the stamp allotment, the purchase requirement determines the amount of subsidy the household receives (the food stamp bonus). As an artifact of basing stamp allotments on least-cost nutritionally adequate diets, the program's benefit schedule specifies purchase requirements below 30% of net income for one- and two-person households, as well as for some very poor eligibles.

As noted earlier, the Ford administration initiated the food stamp debate by proposing a uniform purchase price set at 30% of net income. Opponents of this proposal countered that, despite rhetoric about uniform treatment of all stamp users, the proposal was intended to cut total program expenditures at the cost of reduced benefits for elderly and other relatively less well-off households. If the strategy of proposing a 30% purchase price was intended to focus attention on the program's benefit schedule, it apparently succeeded. As indicated in Table 7.1, both the Senate bill and the House Agriculture Committee bill would institute a uniform purchase requirement. But these bills "hold harmless" small and very poor households by reducing the purchase requirement for all households to 25 and 27.5% of net income, respectively. Although Congress saw merit in uniform treatment for all households, it was opposed to achieving expenditure reductions via increased stamp prices. Thus any congressional cutbacks in program expenditures would presumably derive from other changes.

A Standard Deduction

All three reform bills would have included a standard deduction to replace the existing itemized deductions from the total income of each food stamp household. Since eligibility for the program is based on net income after any deductions, the current deduction system sets the maximum net income allowable for program eligibility. Under each of the reform bills, this procedure would change, in that the maximum income for eligibility would be set at a net income equal to the official poverty threshold plus the standard deduction. Therefore, some recipients with net incomes below the existing maximums would become ineligible under a standard deduction. It is this feature of the standard deduction that is attractive to persons desiring reduced program costs. Initial calculations led the Ford administration to believe that a $100 standard deduction would save $1.2 billion during fiscal 1977 (U.S. House Agriculture Committee, 1976). However, those calculations were later found to overestimate the expected cost savings because preliminary data on the level of deductions taken by reci-

TABLE 7.1
Comparison of Current Program to Reform Agendas

Provisions	Current program	Administration proposed regulations	Senate-passed bill (S. 3136)	House-proposed bill (H.R. 13613)
I. Financial Eligibility Criteria				
Deductions				
Standard	Uses itemized deductions	$100	$100 (except for Puerto Rico, the Virgin Islands, and Guam); adjusted semiannually	$50 for 1-member households; $70 for 2-member households; $90 for 3-member households; $100 for 4-member households; $105 for 5-member households; $110 for households of 6 or more members (except that the Secretary shall determine the standard deduction for American San Guam, Puerto Rico and the Virgin Islands; adjusted semiannually.
Elderly	No specific provision	$25 for any household with at least one member is 65 or older	$25 for any household with at least one member who is 60 or older	$25 for any household with at least one member who is 60 or older

hold may also deduct mandatory deductions such as: local, State and Federal income taxes; social security taxes; retirement payments; union dues; some garnishments

that has at least $150/month in earned income. [Note: no household can claim both this deduction and the deduction for elderly]. A household may also deduct Federal, state and local income taxes and social security taxes paid by employees.

| Other | Allows deduction of: medical costs over $10/month; child or invalid care; tuition and required education fees; unusual expenses (e.g., disaster or theft losses and funeral expenses); support and alimony payments; shelter costs which exceed 30 percent of household income after all other deductions | None | None | None |

113

Table 7.1 (*Continued*)

Provisions	Current program	Administration proposed regulations	Senate-passed bill (S. 3136)	House-proposed bill (H.R. 13613)
Maximum Income *Gross*	No effective gross income limit	4-person, non-elderly working household: $6,696 4-person, non-elderly non-working household: $6,969 1-person, elderly, non-working household: $4,296	4-person, non-elderly working household: $8,160 4-person, non-elderly non-working household: $6,696 1-person, elderly, non-working household: $4,296	4-person, non-elderly, working household: $8,370 4-person, non-elderly, non-working household: $6,696 1-person, elderly, non-working household: $3,696
Net	The point at which the cost of a nutritionally adequate diet equals 30% of net income ($6,636) for a 4-person household; $2,580 for a 1-person household	Nonfarm income poverty guidleines	Nonfarm income poverty guidelines	Nonfarm income poverty guidelines
Accounting *Period*	Counts the income that is anticipated for the period of certification (prior income may be used as a guide)	Counts the average monthly income over the 90 days preceding the month of application ("retrospective accounting"); longer accounting periods for certain households	Counts the income from the 30 days preceding the month of application ("retrospective accounting"); longer accounting periods for certain households; special speeded-up application process for households with a substantial loss	Counts the income that is anticipated for the period of certification; annual income regularly derived in substantially less than a year would be averaged over a 12-month period

Purchase Requirement	Households are charged an amount representing a reasonable investment by the household not to exceed 30 percent of net household income. Four-person households with incomes under $30 per month may be issued coupon allotments without charge. Basis of Issuance tables established by the Secretary determines purchase requirements for individual households	Households shall be charged 30 percent of income as defined by the Regulations	Households shall be charged 25 percent of income as defined by the Act	Households shall be charged 27.5 percent of income as computed in the proposed legislation $10 minimum bonus for 1- and 2-person households; $5 minimum for 3-person households and above

Source: U.S. House Agriculture Committee Staff (1976, pp. 34, 37, 40, 85).

TABLE 7.2
Percentage of Payments Going to Various Poverty Levels under Selected Proposals[a,b]

Current program gross income expressed as a fraction of the poverty level	Current program	S 3136 (Senate-passed bill) (4/8/76)	H.R. 13613	New regulations (5/7/76)
0–1.0	83.6	86.0	87.7	90.9
1.01–1.20	9.6	10.3	9.4	8.0
1.21–1.50	5.2	3.5	2.8	1.0
1.51	1.6	0.2	0.1	0.0

Source: U.S. House Agriculture Committee Staff (1976, p. 10).

[a]Percentages are based upon major eligibility features only. Furthermore, this table does not take into account new households who would join the program under different proposals.

[b]The poverty level used is that which went into effect April 30, 1975 and that which was in effect immediately preceding April 30. The monthly poverty level for a family of four using this calculation would be $400. The fraction of poverty level is calculated as gross income (under current program rules) divided by the poverty level for the appropriate family size.

pients in the existing program overstated the true levels. That is, better data revealed that only a small percentage of current recipients exceed the proposed net income limitations under any of the reform bills.

To illustrate, in Table 7.2 the proportion of payments to persons at various fractions of the poverty threshold declines sharply above that threshold. Only about 15% of all payments go to persons above the poverty line under the current program. Since the net income maximum under the three alternatives exceeds the poverty line in the amount of the proposed standard deduction, it is understandable why those alternatives would not drastically reduce the number of program eligibles.

In conjunction with the Congressional Budget Office, the House Agriculture Committee staff has estimated that a standard deduction would save over $2 million a year in federal administrative costs. Since states bear half the total administrative cost burden of employing caseworkers, this figure presumably accounts for about one-half the total savings due to a standard deduction. Thus administrative cost savings would be substantial.

Because some program eligibles would be made worse off by a standard deduction, one might question whether the associated cost savings outweigh this disadvantage. Table 7.3 provides information to assess this tradeoff, by demonstrating what percentage of recipients would lose or gain specific monthly benefit amounts for each of the reform bills. According to the table, none of the three bills would harm more than one-third of the recipients, and losses would generally be between $5 and 15 dollars per month. A relatively small percentage would lose all benefits or suffer benefit declines in excess of $50 per month. Hence, perhaps the gains in administrative convenience from a standard deduction are justified.

Should there be a standard deduction, the question of its size becomes relevant. Two basic alternatives are presented by the three bills considered here. President Ford's regulations and the Senate-passed bill both adopted a $100 standard deduction with a $25 add-on for households containing elderly persons. Under the House Agriculture Committee bill, the deduction would vary by household size (one-person—$45; two—$55; three—$65; four—$75; five—$80; six or more—$85) in an attempt to set deductions at the average of actual deductions taken by households of each size in the present program. This proposal is desirable, because it accounts for known differences in needs that are associated with household size. In this connection, it should be emphasized that the original intent of deductions from total household income was to account for differences in household needs that result in different amounts of income disposable for food consumption. In the extreme, it can therefore be ar-

TABLE 7.3

Percentage Distribution of All Current Participants Who Gain and Lose under Major Food Stamp Proposals [a]

	New regulations (5/7/76)	S. 3136 (Senate-passed) (4/8/76)	H.R. 13613
Ineligible	4.8	3.9	8.9
Lose > $50	3.1	.3	.6
Lose 49–30	3.9	1.4	2.0
Lose 29–16	8.6	3.2	6.7
Lose 15–5	15.3	9.5	12.9
Total lose, including ineligibles	*35.7*	*18.1*	*31.1*
No change	20.6	17.3	22.0
Gain 5–15	20.5	20.3	18.7
Gain 16–29	22.1	28.9	18.9
Gain 30–49	.9	14.5	8.6
Gain > 50	.0	.8	.7
Total gain	*43.5*	*64.5*	*46.9*
Average Bonus Average Bonus under the current program: $71.11	*$68.26*	*$81.30*	*$73.23*

Source: U.S. House Agriculture Committee Staff (1976, p. 12C).
[a] These percentages are based upon major eligibility features only.

gued that the existing deduction system is superior because it individualizes these needs computations. However, because Congress and the public have clearly demonstrated a concern that this process also generates abuses due to "excessive" deductions, and in view of the evidence that most recipients would not lose substantial benefits, the case for the existing system is not overwhelming. On the other hand, standardizing deductions does not require that we ignore gross differences in needs that are at least partially reflected by household size. For this reason, the House Agriculture Committee proposal deserves special consideration.

However, the committee's standard deduction proposal does not account for regional variation in itemized deductions under the existing program. As summarized in Chapter 2, food stamp recipients with below poverty threshold incomes have average deductions that range from a high of $82 per month in New England to a low of about $54 in the Southeast and mid-Atlantic states. Congressional Budget Office researchers report variation of the same range for recipients above the poverty line, and attribute this to differences in the itemized deduction for shelter costs (Congressional Budget Office, 1976). Although none of the reform bills would regionalize the standard deduction, these findings suggest that such an option deserves attention. Again, the underlying purpose of the deduc- tion system needs to be clarified before deciding whether this option ought to be adopted.

The Accounting Period

To determine benefit entitlements under an income-maintenance program, program regulations specify the period over which a potential recipient's total countable income and expenditure deduction are to be computed. This period is called the accounting period. By contrast, a certification period refers to the length of time a recipient may be eligible to draw benefits, once these benefits are determined.

Both the Ford administration's enjoined regulations and the Senate bill propose a retrospective accounting period. Under retrospective ac- counting, benefit entitlements are determined on the basis of income re- ceived during a period prior to the household's application for program eligibility. The Ford administration proposed a 90-day retrospective ac- counting period, whereas the Senate bill would count income only during the month prior to an application. The House Committee bill would main- tain the current accounting procedure that computes benefits prospectively from a caseworker's forecast of income for the period of intended certifica- tion. Thus under the current system, applicants suffering recent income declines receive benefits that take this decline into account. Under retro- spective accounting, benefits would be calculated on the basis of the larger income flow over prior months. Relative to the present system, then, retro- spective accounting would reduce bonus stamp costs. A disadvantage of this proposal, of course, is that its savings are obtained by reducing benefits for recipients during the early part of a household income setback. On the other hand, at the end of a temporary income decline, households may need substantial aid to augment their incomes after their own assets are depleted; but under prospective accounting caseworkers can then reduce the household's stamp benefits in anticipation of rising household income. For this reason, one might favor retrospective accounting, even apart from expected savings due to reduced stamp payments.

Overall Impact of the Bills

Although the recent interest in reforming food stamps undoubtedly stems from widespread concern about rising program costs, the estimated impact of the three reform bills on total program costs is not large. According to detailed cost estimates of the net impact of all major provisions in each of the three proposals, only the Ford regulations would actually cut program expenditures (see Table 7.4). Moreover, the distribution of benefits among broad classes of recipients would not change very much if any of the three reforms were to be enacted. According to Table 7.5, the percentage of total benefits received by the elderly, the working poor, large families, and by AFDC recipients would remain about the same as under the current program. Of course, some individuals would gain or lose benefits. But on the whole, none of the three reforms represents a drastic departure from the current program's total cost and benefit distribution.

TABLE 7.4
Cost Estimates of Major Food Stamp Bills Fiscal Year 1977 (in billions)

	Current program	New regulations (5/7/76)	S. 3136 (Senate-passed) (4/8/76)	H.R. 13613
Total costs	6.179	5.745	7.140	6.479
Administrative costs	.404	.376	.422	.420

Source: U.S. House Agriculture Committee Staff (1976, p. 2).

TABLE 7.5
Distribution of Food Stamp Bonus Dollars by Selected Characteristics under Major Food Stamp Proposals (in percentage of total bonus dollars)

	Current Program	New Regulations (5/7/76)	S. 3136 (Senate-passed-bill) (4/8/76)	H.R. 13613
Elderly	17.8	22.6	22.2	20.5
Working poor	25.4	21.2	23.6	25.1
AFDC	49.7	51.9	51.2	51.3
Large families	42.7	42.0	42.1	45.9

Source: U.S. House Agriculture Committee Staff (1976, p. 10).

Apparently, Congress has rejected the clamor for a major food stamp cutback. In turn, this may imply that proposals intended to further expand the program deserve consideration.

It is unlikely that any legislation to expand the program would be enacted without simultaneous adoption of changes intended to streamline program operations. Therefore, we might expect to see a standard deduction and/or a retrospective accounting period enacted. Whether or not Congress will alter the program's benefit schedule depends on many factors, including the extent of support for enrolling new recipients.

EXPANSION PROPOSALS

An expanded program would fortify the unique role of food stamps in our present income-maintenance system. The most important aspects of this role are that the stamps reduce interstate differentials in combined benefits for welfare recipients; they primarily benefit households with incomes below the official poverty line; and they assist the working poor. Further gains along these lines are possible, because the current program has a relatively low participation rate.

Two methods of expansion are described and compared here—elimination of the purchase requirement (EPR) and replacing bonus stamps with cash transfers. Both methods would increase potential recipients' satisfaction from using food stamps, thereby encouraging increased participation.

Elimination of the Purchase Requirement

Under EPR, all recipients would receive their bonus food stamps free of charge. Thus although a household would get fewer total food stamps under this proposal, it would get the same number of bonus stamps. A provision to this effect was narrowly defeated in Senate Committee hearings when Senator Talmadge chose not to break a 7−7 tie vote. To evaluate EPR, we consider whom it might attract to the program, the extent of its disadvantages for persons favoring in-kind aid, and the size of its expected addition to total program costs.

An EPR would raise the cash equivalent value of bonus stamps. This value depends on the relationship between desired food expenditures and those that are required of program participants. Enacting EPR would reduce required food expenditures, because the current program requires recipients to spend the stamp allotment (or some quarter fraction thereof), whereas EPR only constrains the recipient to spend the stamp bonus on food. Therefore EPR would partially relax the program's constraint on household expenditure allocation, such that recipients could devote a smaller proportion of their budget to food, increasing the cash equivalent value of the stamps.

According to estimates derived by Smeeding (1977) an EPR would raise the cash value of a bonus stamp dollar to the average recipient from 90 cents to 96 cents. Because very low-income households now have relatively low cash equivalent ratios, Smeeding's estimated increase stems primarily from increased cash equivalent values among relatively poor recipients. Among existing recipients, then, EPR appears to be most favorable for the very needy.

It is difficult to anticipate with certainty what kinds of eligible nonparticipants would choose to participate if bonus stamps were provided free of charge. If the purchase requirement confuses eligibles, an EPR might reduce information costs, attracting many uninformed eligibles. However, as suggested by Chapter 6, the characteristics of uninformed eligibles are largely unknown. Considering informed nonparticipants, the effects of an EPR depend on how these households currently value bonus stamps. It seems reasonable to assume that nonparticipants value bonus stamps even less than participants. Extending Smeeding's finding that relatively poor recipients would benefit most from an EPR, it is to be expected that relatively poor nonrecipients would be attracted to the program.

For persons favoring food stamps as a nutritional assistance device, or to strengthen the demand for food, eliminating the purchase requirement would weaken the already indirect link between the program's effects on recipient behavior and food consumption (or nutritional status). Food-nutrition advocates would expect that such a reformed program would be less nutritionally effective, since recipients would no longer be required to surrender cash for food vouchers. Moreover, should these same persons oppose cash transfers, they would tend not to favor "free" stamps, because of their similarity to cash transfers.

Yet if the findings of Chapter 3 are correct, those misgivings are partially unfounded, because the program already acts much like a cash transfer program—that is, it increases general purchasing power, with some habitual fraction of that increase spent on food. The most compelling evidence in favor of this conclusion is surprisingly simple, and therefore quite plausible—most recipients spend more on food than is required in spending their entire stamp allotment. In addition, Chapter 4 found that increasing general purchasing power is not very cost effective for improving nutritional status. Instead, nutrition advocates should prefer programs that establish direct links to nutritional intake.

Because handling and controlling the cash paid by recipients for stamps is a costly process, an EPR would provide some administrative cost savings. However, these savings would almost certainly be outweighed by rising subsidy payments as program participation responds to greater cash equivalent values. The Congressional Budget Office (1976) has estimated, under reasonable assumptions, that participation would increase between 10 and 20% as a result of an EPR. In fiscal year 1978, such increases would boost program costs by between $600 million and $1.2 billion. Assuming the larger cost increase, the EPR might therefore raise program costs by roughly 20% of the fiscal 1977 program budget.

If the public and Congress are willing to accept these increased costs, along with the associated program emphasis on income supplementation, another alternative might also be considered—replacing bonus stamps with cash.

A Cash Out

Although Congress has never seriously considered providing cash in lieu of bonus stamps as a food stamp reform alternative, a "cash out" does seem to be a logical extension of the reasoning behind the EPR proposal. Moreover, as discussed in Chapter 1, the Congress did give serious consideration to President Nixon's Family Assistance Plan, which was originally intended to replace food stamps and other welfare programs with cash transfers for families. Although comprehensive negative income tax plans of this type certainly represent an alternative to the current food stamp program, evaluating such plans is beyond the scope of our discussion. Instead, we consider cash transfers for food stamp eligibles, assuming other welfare programs would continue.

The major distinction between an EPR and a cash out is that the EPR would preserve the "near cash" aspects of the existing program without explicitly authorizing a cash program. Thus, for purposes of political compromise, an EPR offers a decided advantage over a cash out. However, program eligibles would undoubtedly prefer a cash out, since this step would end any stigma attached to the use of stamps, and simultaneously raise cash equivalent values. Therefore if the stamps were cashed out, program participation would almost certainly exceed participation under the EPR alternative.

Difficulties in quantifying the inhibiting effect of stigma (if any) on participation prevent exact estimation of the increment in program costs that would be associated with a cash out. Yet if we assume that participation would rise to the 90% participation rate estimated for the Aid to Families with Dependent Children program, estimates from the Congressional Budget Office provide a standard for comparison with the incremental costs of an EPR. According to these estimates, cashing out food stamps would raise program costs by $2.2 to $2.7 billion. Based on the highest cost estimates for both alternatives, this implies that cash out would cost $1.5 billion a year more than EPR. In terms of recipient benefits, the expenditure of this extra sum would represent a substantial contribution toward improving the well-being of low-income families.

With respect to preserving work incentives, although food stamps might lead to some increase in welfare dependency in lieu of gainful work, this effect need not be large, for two reasons. First, the maximum stamp benefit—available when the household has no other income—does not dominate incomes available to households working at low (say, legal minimum) wages. Second, the rate at which food stamp benefits are reduced as earnings rise is roughly 30% of net income, which allows working poor households to retain the bulk of their earnings. Moreover, as summarized in Chapter 5, the results of negative income tax experiments suggest that providing benefits in this fashion does not interfere with recipients' commitment to work.

On the whole, then, cashing out food stamps would simply redistribute more income, at substantially greater cost, than EPR would. Hence the choice between these two proposals depends very much on the extent to which taxpayers are willing to donate income, in any form, to program eligibles.

SUMMARY

During and after the most recent economic recession, rising enrollment in the food stamp program alarmed fiscal conservatives, drawing their attention to the regulations on food stamp benefits and eligibility. Hence in January, 1976, the Ford administration initiated a prolonged debate over reforming program regulations. Of the three most prominent reform agendas subsequently considered by President Ford and the 94th Congress, only the administration's proposed regulations would actually reduce program expenditures. This reduction would be accomplished by increasing the price of food stamps for some recipients, reducing administrative costs with a standard deduction, and by decreasing benefits via a 90-day retrospective accounting period. By contrast, a modest rise in total program cost is to be expected if either the House Committee or Senate-passed bill is enacted. The more liberal Senate bill would maintain the current accounting procedures for determining benefits, and reduce purchase prices to 25% of net income. The House Committee proposals would set purchase prices at 27.5% of net income and would institute a 30-day retrospective accounting period. Retrospective accounting works to the disadvantage of households during the early part of a period of temporary income decline, but is more favorable than current procedures when household incomes return to their predecline levels. On balance, however, retrospective accounting is thought to reduce benefit payments relative to the current procedures.

Both congressional bills would institute a standard deduction, but the House version specifies standard deductions that increase with household size, reflecting deductions taken on average under the current program. Thus the House deduction proposal has the advantage of maintaining national average deductions, while capturing administrative cost savings from streamlining the benefit determination procedure. Due to regional variations in shelter costs, instituting any uniform deduction procedure would lead to fewer benefits for recipients in high shelter cost areas. Yet on the whole, estimates prepared by the House Agriculture Committee staff suggest that a relatively small percentage of all recipients stand to lose all benefits or suffer benefit declines in excess of $50 per month from instituting any of the three reform agendas. Hence although these three agendas would alter program regulations in significant ways, they do not represent a drastic cutback in program benefits.

Nor do these agendas represent any change in the existing program's ability to provide assistance for needy households, which is limited by the reluctance of nonparticipants, who comprise about half of the program's eligible population. Because the Food Stamp Program could fill this and other gaps in the present federal system for income support, and since there is widespread concern for improving that system, we also considered the Dole–McGovern proposal to provide bonus stamps free of charge, in contrast with the oft-mentioned option to replace bonus stamps with equivalent cash payments. The main merit (or disadvantage, depending on how one values income redistribution in any form) of both proposals is that they would tend to increase program enrollment by raising the cash equivalent value of benefits for recipients. At the same time, either move would constitute explicit Congressional approval of the current program's primary role as a provider of income assistance—the more so if the stamps were cashed out. The associated costs and benefits of operating a cash transfer program via the existing food stamp delivery system are expected to substantially exceed those from eliminating purchase requirements, on the assumption that eligibles prefer cash to stamps.

At present, it is difficult to determine how taxpayers feel about the two alternatives. We do know that prominent senators have endorsed free food stamps, and that the Congress nearly adopted the Family Assistance Plan, which would have provided more generous benefits to all eligible families than are currently available from food stamps. At any rate, because the Food Stamp Program has the potential for accomplishing further income redistribution, while targeting benefits primarily to officially poor households, proposals to expand the program deserve serious consideration. An advantage of debating the relative merits of free food stamps versus a cash out would be a clarification of our values toward income transfers, in the context of the related choice between providing income in cash or in-kind.

Epilogue

This book has presented a discussion and analysis of the Food Stamp program—its objectives, its effects, its problems, and suggestions for reform. As of September 1977, legislative passage and presidential approval of a major reform of the Food Stamp program seem virtually certain. It is thus appropriate to append a short epilogue describing the changes this legislation will bring about, within the context of the overall discussion in the body of the book.

Elimination of the Purchase Requirement. Under previous legislation, there was a food stamp purchase requirement. This meant that before all but the very poorest families could receive any bonus stamps, they had to produce a certain minimum amount of cash to pay for them. The new legislation eliminates the purchase requirements, so that in the future no one will be prevented from using food stamps because they lack the minimum cash necessary to pay for them. (The number of stamps, and therefore the generosity of the benefit, will still depend on household income and household size.)

Predictions are that the new legislative action will increase the number of persons who will participate in the program. By simplifying the program rules it may also attract people who are currently eligible but do not understand the program rules sufficiently to apply. This simplification can also be expected to reduce the administrative costs of the program.

Other probable effects, however, will be regarded by some as less favorable. Program costs will probably increase by an amount that will substantially outweigh the administrative cost savings mentioned above. Eliminating the purchase requirement will further weaken the likelihood that the program will increase the total expenditures on food by recipient households. (To the extent that recipients are already unconstrained in their expenditure choices, which the available evidence appears to suggest, this will not be an important factor.)

Congress is sensitive to the possible participation and cost impacts of the change. It has, therefore, directed the Secretary of Agriculture to provide special reports to Congress on these issues—the first report due 6 months after enactment, subsequent ones to be due annually.

REDUCTION OF INCOME ELIGIBILITY LIMITS

Under previous program rules, the net income eligibility limits were higher than the official poverty line, which varies according to family size. In addition, there were numerous complicated deductions allowable in computing net income for eligibility purposes. Some households above the poverty line, as a result, were eligible for and took advantage of the Food Stamp program. The new legislation tackles both problems.

First, it sets a firm net income limit for eligibility to coincide with the official poverty thresholds. This means, for example, that the net income limit for a household of four will be $5850, to be adjusted annually for cost of living increases.

Second, the allowable deductions from gross income have been simplified, which should lower administrative costs as well as the effective net income limit. A monthly standard deduction of $60 per household is allowed. Only three specific allowable deductions remain: (1) a 20% earned income deduction, (2) a dependent care deduction, and (3) a shelter cost deduction for those paying over 50% of their income on shelter. A maximum limit of $75 per month has been instituted for combined day care and shelter costs.[1]

---

[1]This amount is the result of a political compromise between representatives from low versus high shelter cost areas.

PILOT TESTS OF A STRONGER WORK PROVISION

The previous legislation required all able-bodied, nonaged adults in a household (except those responsible for care of dependents, students, and persons working at least 30 hours a week) to register for employment. They were, in addition, required to accept "reasonable" offers of employment or lose household eligibility for a year. The new legislation requires each of the 7 USDA regional districts to conduct 2 pilot projects—one in an urban, one in a rural area—to test a mandatory work provision. In these pilots, work registrants not obtaining work in the private sector within 30 days will be required to accept public service employment and will be paid in the form of their food stamp allotments. Clearly, the intent of this experimentation is to pave the way for possible strengthening of the work tests in the Food Stamp program as a whole.

There are, in addition, new provisions to tie student eligibility to work activity, such that only students who (1) are registered for work or work at least half time, or (2) are heads of households with dependents remain eligible—and then only provided they are not or could not be claimed as tax dependents by parents who are themselves ineligible for the stamps.

INCENTIVES TO IMPROVE PROGRAM ADMINISTRATION

According to available quality control figures on the Food Stamp program, about 28% of the total monthly bonus dollars issued in food stamps under the old administrative system and rules were issued incorrectly. Most of the errors were connected with overissuing stamps (including to ineligibles). More than 10%, however, were underissue cases. The new legislation includes stronger positive incentives for efficient administration, as well as stronger penalties for laxity.

The federal matching of administrative costs associated with investigation and prosecution of fraud is raised from 50 to 75% under the new law. Also, states which reduce certification error rates below 10% will have the federal matching of their overall administrative costs raised from 50 to 60%. Those which reduce error rates below 5% will have their federal matching share raised to 65%.

On the penalty side, states that do not comply with federal standards, according to the new law, will have the matching of their administrative costs reduced as deemed appropriate by the Secretary of Agriculture. So far there has been no provision for reducing matching shares. The new legislation also requires the Department of Agriculture to establish staffing patterns at the state level that will ensure proper program administration.

CARTER'S WELFARE REFORM PACKAGE

As this goes to press, Congress is preparing to consider President Carter's comprehensive welfare reform package, which includes a provision to replace food stamps entirely with cash supplements. Such cashing out, of course, would eliminate the whole Food Stamp program and break completely any tie between assistance and incentives to increase or improve food consumption per se. According to available evidence, however, as I have argued in this book, the current Food Stamp program already acts much like a cash transfer program, increasing general purchasing power. And elimination of the purchase requirement will fortify this role.

The fate of welfare reform this time around will not be decided, in any case, for many months. Even if the proposed legislation passes, it will not be implemented for several years. Therefore the new reforms of the Food Stamp program are still important in their own right.

APPENDIX A

Estimation of the Cash Equivalent Value of Bonus Food Stamps

PRE- AND POSTSTAMP BUDGET CONSTRAINTS

Figure A.1 displays budget constraints faced by households eligible for the Food Stamp program. Distance OC on the vertical axis represents the quantity of goods other than food consumed at home that can be consumed if the household spends its entire prestamp income on these other goods. Similarly, on the horizontal axis, OD represents the maximum quantity of food consumed at home that is obtainable from prestamp income. Therefore, the line CAD represents the prestamp budget constraint, as in the standard indifference curve diagram. We shall now demonstrate how eligible households can use the food stamp program to maximize their set of attainable consumption opportunities.

First, consider how consumption opportunities are expanded when the household buys an entire stamp allotment in 1 month. Distance CM represents the full purchase price of the allotment, and AB represents the resulting amount of bonus food stamps. After this exchange, the household's poststamp budget constraint is represented by the line segments

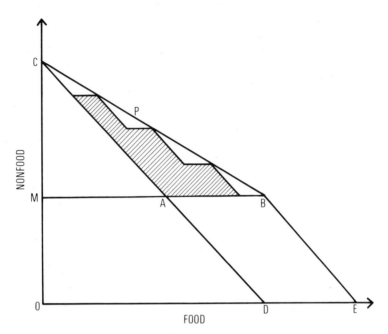

Figure A.1. *Pre- and poststamp budget constraints.*

joining points *C, A, B,* and *E,* and the household gains the opportunity to consume the bundles of goods signified by points in the area bounded by line segments joining *A, B, D,* and *E.*

Using the variable purchase option, the household can further expand its consumption opportunities to include all bundles in the shaded area bounded by the "sawtooth" line segment. This is accomplished by paying some quarter fraction of the full purchase price to get a corresponding quarter fraction of the entire stamp bonus. Since in any given month the household can choose its desired quarter fraction, it can obtain all of the goods bundles in the shaded area.

Furthermore, over an extended period, say 1 year, the household can time its stamp purchases and expenditures to expand its opportunities to include all points within the area bounded by line segments connecting points *C, B,* and *E.* This is possible because households can vary the amount of stamps purchased from month to month and because stamps purchased in one month can be spent in subsequent months. An example helps to clarify this point. Suppose the household buys one-half of the entire bonus one month and one-fourth of the bonus the next month, perhaps saving some of the bonus stamps purchased in the first month for use in the second month. Thus, over the 2 month period the household manages to obtain three-eighths of the available bonus, symbolized by point *P* in the diagram. Over a longer period, as the number of possible stamp transactions rises, the household can buy any fraction of the total bonus available during that same extended period. Hence, the relevant poststamp budget constraint for a food stamp eligible household is *CBE*.

Relative to a cash transfer in amount *AB,* the potential for food stamps to constrain recipient households arises because a cash transfer allows the household to obtain more consumption bundles, that is, "points" outside the area bounded by *CBE*. In Figure A.2, the postcash budget constraint is

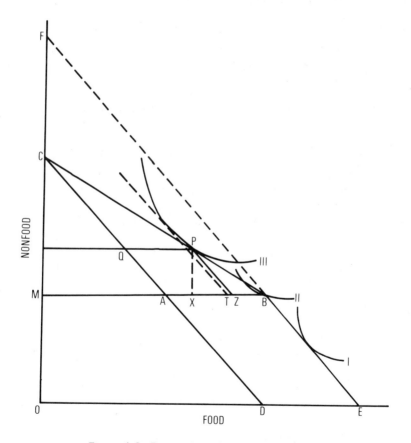

Figure A.2. *Deriving lower-bound cash equivalents.*

represented by the line connecting *F, B,* and *E.* Relative to the poststamp constraint, this postcash constraint expands the set of consumption opportunities to include all points in the area bounded by the triangle *CFB.* Provided some stamp recipients would prefer goods bundles within *CFB* to other available bundles, the in-kind transfer must constrain recipient consumption behavior relative to cash. Note also that another way to view the effect of the in-kind transfer is to recognize that the program offers a food price subsidy for those whose food expenditures are constrained. In other words, the slope of line *CB* represents reduced food prices, relative to the prestamp situation.

At this point, it is useful to reconsider the three kinds of recipients defined in Table 3.1 (see page 54). Recall that recipients who buy more food than that made available by spending the entire stamp allotment (Group I) are not constrained by the program. In terms of Figure A.2, these recipients maximize their satisfaction by choosing a package of goods on line *BE,* as represented by the tangency of indifference curve I to this line. Another group (Group II) consumes food in an amount equal to the stamp allotment, demonstrating the choice of goods bundle represented by point *B.* Except in the event that these households would prefer bundle *B* irrespective of the form of the transfer (in which case the indifference curve would be tangent to line *FBE* at point *B*), these households would choose bundle *B* on an indifference curve like II. Clearly, the substitution of AB in cash for *AB* in bonus stamps would allow these Group II households to obtain greater satisfaction than indicated by indifference curve II. The final group (Group III) consumes less food than it could if it bought the entire stamp bonus. These constrained households would choose some bundle on line *CB.* The figure depicts such a choice. Goods bundle *P* maximizes a Group III household's satisfaction at a level indicated by indifference curve III, which is made possible by bonus stamps in an amount represented by *QP.*

CASH EQUIVALENT VALUES

To derive the cash equivalent value of *QP,* one must determine how much cash the recipient would be willing to trade for *QP* bonus stamps. The minimum amount of cash that would be required is an amount that would make the recipient at least as well off as the food stamps do. Following the standard graphical treatment of cash equivalent values, the necessary cash amount is depicted by *AT.* Because distance *AZ* equals *QP,* the corresponding ratio of this cash equivalent to the bonus value is AT/AZ. In practice, accurate empirical estimation of AT requires that we know the exact form of the recipients' utility function. Most empirical studies of cash equivalent values assume knowledge of this form, by specifying a utility function. However, our procedure is to compute a lower-bound estimate of the true cash equivalent value, without using a utility function. After describing this procedure and its results, we compare our findings to other estimates of cash equivalent food stamp values.

Method and Data

In reference to Figure A.2, we need to estimate AT/AZ. A lower-bound estimate would be AX/AZ, where AX is the extra food consumption attributable to food stamps, relative to the purchase price of the entire stamp allotment, MA. By this method, we take advantage of the presumption that households would not choose to pay more for their entire stamp allotment than they would spend on food under the program. Thus MX, the amount spent on food, will exceed MA, the full cost of the stamp allotment, and $MX - MA$ $(=AX)$ measures only part of the cash equivalent benefit obtained from using food stamps, AT. (When food and nonfood are very good substitutes, it is possible that AX may overestimate AT. However, near subsistence levels, we would not expect a high degree of substitutionability.) The AX values can be computed for sample households from the Michigan Panel Study of Income Dynamics (Morgan *et al.*, 1972).

The 1975 wave of this Panel Study obtained information about 1974 food stamp usage, asking:

How much did you pay for the stamps in 1974 (per week, month)?

How much could you buy with the stamps in 1974 (per week, month)?

As explained in Chapter 3, variables created from the responses to these questions, along with reported food expenditures, allowed us to allocate each recipient household among Groups I, II, and III. For Group I households, the true cash equivalent ratio is known to be 1.00. Lower-bound estimates of the ratios for members of Groups II and III were used to compute an overall weighted average cash equivalent ratio.

Lower-bound estimates for Group II cannot be computed by the method just described, because that method works only when total food expenditures are *less than* the stamp allotment; Group II households had food expenditures *equal to* the stamp allotment. Therefore, lower-bound

TABLE A.1

Estimated Lower Bound Cash Equivalent Ratios and the Percentage Distribution of Recipients; by Income and Household Size; for Constrained[a] Households, 1974 (N = 239)

1974 annual income	Household size							
	1–2		3–4		5–6		7 or More	
	Ratio	Percentage	Ratio	Percentage	Ratio	Percentage	Ratio	Percentage
Less than $2400	.65	8.4	.60	4.7	.62	1.7	.54	2.2
$2400–4799	.82	5.0	.54	9.2	.76	5.8	.65	4.2
$4800–7199	.88	3.4	.67	12.2	.55	8.5	.76	7.6
$7200–8999	.86	2.0	.82	3.3	.81	4.2	.78	2.9
$9000 or more	.94	1.9	.92	1.9	.90	5.9	.87	5.0

[a]Percentage distribution is for Group II and Group III households combined. Some Group II households may actually be unconstrained. However, for estimation purposes we have assumed that lower bound cash equivalent ratio estimates for Group III apply to corresponding income-household size cells for Group II.

ratios for Group II were assumed to equal the estimates computed for Group III households of the same income and household size. The AX values for Group III were calculated by subtracting estimated purchase prices for the entire monthly stamp allotment from the 1974 monthly food expenditure estimate. Because the purchase price depends on net income after allowable deductions, information about average total deductions by income–household size group was obtained from a USDA survey of recipient households (Forscht and Platt, 1976). The use of these average deduction values necessitated computation of average AX values, based on average total income for 20 income–household size groups.

Table A.1 presents the resulting lower-bound cash equivalent ratios for Groups II and III by income and household size, along with the percentage distribution of these recipient households among the 20 cells of the table. Generally, cash equivalent ratios rise with income and decline with household size. Apparently, stamp allotments substantially exceed desired food expenditures among small and very low-income households. As will be demonstrated, these relationships have also been observed in other studies. Weighting the cell cash-equivalent ratios according to the proportion of all households in each cell produced a weighted average cash equivalent ratio of .72, indicating that, on average, over two-thirds of the subsidy obtained by constrained households can be spent freely. Moreover, the weighted average cash-equivalent ratio for the entire recipient sample was .92, reflecting the relatively greater frequency of unconstrained participants. On the whole then, our estimates suggest food stamps are very much like cash, from the recipients' standpoint.

Other Studies

To provide an informed perspective on our estimated cash equivalent ratios, in this section, we survey other pertinent studies. Some of these studies are also summarized by Janis Peskin (1976).

Table A.2 presents estimated cash equivalent ratios from a study by Kenneth W. Clarkson (1976), "Welfare Benefits of the Food Stamp Program." Clarkson assumes that all recipient households buy the entire stamp bonus, and that these households spend no more or less than the full allotment on food. In other words, Clarkson assumed that all recipients

TABLE A.2

Estimates of Cash Equivalent to Bonus Value Ratios by Income Class and Household Size for June 1973

Monthly income	Household size					
	1	2	3	4	5	6
Under $29	.60	.45	.40	.36	.33	.30
$30–39	.82	.65	.56	.50	.45	.42
$40–49	.90	.70	.60	.54	.50	.46
$50–69	.97	.77	.65	.57	.55	.50
$70–99	.99	.85	.74	.67	.62	.57
$100–149	1.00	.99	.84	.78	.71	.66
$150–249	—	1.00	.95	.91	.85	.80
$250–359	—	—	1.00	.99	.97	.94
$360–419	—	—	—	1.00	1.00	.99
$420–479	—	—	—	—	1.00	1.00
$480–539	—	—	—	—	—	1.00

Source: Derived from Clarkson (1976, p. 869).

behave like members of Group II. Relative to our estimates, Clarkson's procedure tends to introduce biases in estimated cash equivalent values for Groups I and III. He specified a Cobb–Douglas utility function, from which an indirect utility function was derived to allow computation of the cash equivalent value of the entire stamp bonus available to recipients. A key assumption for this computation was that all households had the same marginal propensity to consume food, .33. Evidence from the New Jersey Negative Income Tax Experiment (Nicholson, 1973) suggests that low-income households may actually have lower marginal propensities to consume food, in the range of .7–.18. Clarkson reports that most budgetary studies of the poor indicate that .33 is a mean value.

According to these findings, cash equivalent values rise with income and decline with household size. When the results for the income–household-size groups in Table A.2 were weighted according to relative frequencies of program participation, the average cash equivalent ratio was found to be .83. Apparently, Clarkson's assumption that all recipient households obtain the entire stamp bonus and spend no more than the stamp allotment on food leads to an overall cash equivalent ratio estimate that is substantially below our lower-bound estimate.

An advantage of another study, by Eugene Smolensky *et al.* (1974) is that cash equivalents of food stamps for prototype recipient households were estimated both with and without accounting for in-kind benefits other than food stamps, using a variant of the displaced CES utility function. In other words, Smolensky *et al.* performed some simulations based on a more comprehensive definition of household income, allowing for multiple benefit packages that included public housing, rent supplements, Medicare, and Medicaid. This procedure accounts for the possibility that other in-kind benefits might allow some food stamp recipient households to choose freely to devote more income to food than required in spending the entire stamp allotment. None of the simulations performed by Smolensky *et al.* produced cash equivalent to bonus values below .8. In part, this result stems from their use of relatively well-off prototype recipient households. Nevertheless, it is useful to know that simulations based on a more comprehensive income definition and a different specification of the utility function lead to findings that are generally similar to those of the Clarkson study.

Timothy Smeeding (1975) used an alternative method to establish lower bounds for the cash equivalent value of bonus food stamps. This method does not simulate utility maximization. Instead, food stamp allotments for recipient households are compared to food expenditures of demographically similar nonparticipant households, whose total income equals the recipient households' combined cash and bonus food stamp income. By this method, recipients are found to be constrained by the program when their food expenditures exceed that of nonrecipients at comparable income levels (assuming all household have the same preferences for food). When nonrecipient expenditures were below the stamp allotment for recipients at comparable income levels, Smeeding employed a technique similar to our method to produce an estimate for the cash equivalent value of the entire stamp bonus. (Recall that our estimates are for the bonus actually received by recipients.)

Table A.3 contains Smeeding's estimates for various income classes. The overall average ratio of cash equivalents to bonus values was .89, rising by income class from .73, below $1000, to 1.00 at $6000 in annual income. Given that Smeeding's estimation method is more like ours than were the methods of the other studies, and that our estimate is quite close to Smeeding's, the two estimates appear to corroborate each other.

In another study, Malcom Galatin (1973) applied a variant of Smeeding's method, comparing food stamp allotment amounts to food expenditures expected for categories of cash transfer recipients on the basis of typical benefit levels. Galatin estimated that the cash equivalent to bonus value ratio was 1.00 for 23% of couples receiving old age assistance; 76% of single-person old age assistance recipients; 31% of two-person AFDC units; none of the four-person AFDC units.

TABLE A.3
Recipient Valuation of Food Stamp Bonus Values, 1972

Disposable personal income	Average annual bonus value	Average annual cash equivalent	Cash equivalent to bonus value ratio
$0–999	$659	481	.73
1000–1999	343	295	.86
2000–2999	297	261	.88
3000–3999	355	316	.89
4000–4999	344	310	.90
5000–5999	334	309	.93
6000–7499	344	325	.95
7500–9999	325	323	1.00
10,000+	375	375	1.00

Source: Derived from Smeeding (1975, p. 357).

In a study of the impact of the food stamp program on the demand for food, Mittlehammer and West (1974) provide further evidence that bonus values are equivalent to cash, especially at incomes close to the maximums for eligibility.

An unfortunate aspect of the studies reviewed here is that they are based on Consumer Expenditure Survey data collected in 1960–1961. If the proportion of income spent on food has changed significantly, the findings from those studies could be misleading. In this connection, it should be emphasized that our estimates rely on food expenditure reports collected in 1975 from food stamp recipients.

Some circumstantial evidence is available from one other study relying on recent food expenditure reports from the data set that was used in our estimations. In a study designed to predict the influence of income from various sources on food expenditures, Saul Hymans and Harold Shapiro (1974) estimated marginal propensities to consume (MPC) food out of bonus food stamp income, for a sample of all households with the same head and spouse during the first 5 years of the *Michigan Panel Study of Income Dynamics* (1967–1972). Before discussing their findings, let us review what the MPC is, and how MPC measures for food can add to the evidence about the extent to which food stamps constrain recipient consumption behavior.

The MPC is an increment in consumption attributable to an increment in income, expressed as a percentage of that increment in income. Thus, the MPC food out of bonus food stamp income measures the increment in food expenditures due to the use of bonus food stamps, as a percentage of some change in bonus food stamp income. Since the MPC food out of bonus stamp income conveys no information about what food amounts would be consumed if cash were provided instead of stamps, this MPC measure cannot be used by itself to infer anything about cash equivalent values. In other words, simply observing what proportion of an increment to the stamp bonus is devoted to food tells us nothing about what would happen if a face-value equivalent increment in cash were received, and we need to know the latter to measure cash equivalents.

However, by comparing an MPC measure for bonus stamp income to the MPC food out of cash income, we can at least determine whether food stamps do constrain recipient consumption behavior. If they do, we would expect to find that the MPC food out of stamps exceeds that for cash. Indeed, as shown in Table A.4 this is what Hymans and Shapiro found. It appears that food stamps lead to roughly 20% more food consumption than cash transfer payments taking the form of welfare income. With re-

TABLE A.4

Marginal Propensity to Consume Food from Various Income Sources

	Wage income	Welfare income	Other transfer income	Income from food subsidy program	
				Urban households	Nonurban households
Target households[a]	.143	.184	.141	.347	.541
Nontarget households	.046	.087	.047	.250	.444

Source: Hymans and Shapiro (1974, p. 267).

[a]Households comprising the lowest quintile on the average ratio of income-food needs, for the first five years of the panel (1968–1972), where food needs are measured by the U.S. Department of Agriculture's Economy Diet Plan, in 1967 prices.

spect to estimates of cash equivalent values, this evidence does establish that, on average, food stamp recipients are constrained by the program.

Thus the Hymans and Shapiro study corroborates the conclusion that food stamps do restrict consumption behavior, consistent with our estimate that the cash equivalent to bonus value ratio for the stamps is less than 1.00.

In summary, there appears to be general agreement among available findings that food stamps do not greatly constrain the average recipient household's consumption behavior. These same studies also indicate that households of smaller size and relatively lower income do tend to be more constrained than on average.

APPENDIX B

Tables on Food Stamps and the Income-Maintenance System

The following tables provide the basis for much of the analysis presented in Chapter 5 of the role of food stamps in the income-maintenance system. That analysis and these appendix tables assume that a bonus food stamp is valued the same as a dollar in cash, such that one can add bonus stamp amounts and family income to produce a better measure of total family income. This procedure permits an assessment of the contribution of the Food Stamp program to the income of various types of households.

The first two tables provide a useful description of food stamp households, based on the first comprehensive study of those households. These data were collected by the U.S. Bureau of the Census (1976a, 1976b) in a special addition to the Current Population Survey, which obtains a representative sample of the total population.

Tables B-3 through B-5 were derived by the author from tables published by the U.S. Congress, Joint Economic Committee, and from the June 1973 Current Population Survey tape. They are designed to allow comparisons of both total amounts and sources of benefits for households who obtained income from more than one income transfer program. Figures from these tables compare total household income to the official poverty threshold suitable for determining how certain multiple benefit combinations provide adequate incomes. In addition, data were obtained to permit an estimate of the extent to which food stamps augment incomes available from other sources, and to suggest how well the program fills gaps in coverage for the entire income maintenance system.

TABLE B.1

Characteristics of Food Stamp Households and of Families and Unrelated Individuals below Poverty Level

Characteristics	Households purchasing food stamps November, 1974	Families below poverty level in 1974	Unrelated individuals below poverty level in 1974
Residence			
Nonfarm	97.3	93.3	97.6
Metropolitan	64.3	60.1	64.3
In central city	43.4	35.8	39.0
Outside central city	20.9	24.4	25.3
Nonmetropolitan	33.0	39.9	35.7
Farm	2.7	6.7	2.4
Region			
Northeast	22.3	18.0	22.0
North Central	21.6	20.0	23.2
South	40.5	45.4	36.3
West	15.6	16.6	18.4
Age of Head			
Under 35 years	34.5	39.4	—
35−54 years	34.8	34.3	—
55−64 years	11.6	11.4	—
65 years and over	19.1	14.9	—
Sex of Head			
Male	41.4	54.0	33.3
Female	58.6	46.0	66.7
Race of Head			
White	62.0	68.2	78.3
Nonwhite	38.0	31.8	21.7
Size of household or family			
One	24.7	—	—
Two	21.0	33.4	—
Three	15.5	19.0	—
Four	12.3	16.5	—
Five	9.1	12.0	—
Six	6.4	8.1	—
Seven or more	9.6	11.0	—
(Average size)	(3.2)	(3.4)	
Total number (in thousands)	3971	5109	4820

Source: U.S. Bureau of the Census (1976a, 1976b).

TABLE B.2

Percentages of Families and Unrelated Individuals below the Poverty Level Not Purchasing Food Stamps in 1974, by Characteristic

	Families
Race	
White	66.7%
Black	42.8
Sex of head	
Male	73.8
Female	42.0
Age of head	
Under 35 years	36.9
35 to 44 years	41.8
55 to 64 years	53.2
65 years and over	75.3
Size of family	
Two persons	72.6
Three	62.4
Four	50.8
Five	50.3
Six	48.0
Seven or more	45.9
Employment status of head	
Employed	76.2
Unemployed	47.1
Not in civilian labor force	48.5
Percentage of all poor families not purchasing stamps	*59.6*
Total number of families below poverty level (in thousands)	*5109*
	Unrelated individuals
Sex	
Male	83.5
Female	78.7
Age	
Under 35 years	59.6
35 to 54 years	86.1
55 to 64 years	73.0
65 years and over	14.3
Total number of unrelated individuals below poverty level (in thousands)	*4820*

Source: U.S. Bureau of the Census (1976b).

TABLE B.3

Monthly Public Benefits,[a] Private Income, and Total Income per Person, for Food Stamps Households in November 1973, by Various Program Combinations

Benefit in combination with food stamps[b]	Percentage of all food stamp households	Average number of persons per household	Public benefits per person	Private income per person	Total income per person
No other program	6.2	2.5	$19.02	$67.11	$86.13
Social Security	10.1	1.6	108.91	15.73	124.64
Social Security and Medicare	3.9	1.5	136.61	10.86	147.47
General Assistance	2.4	2.0	88.25	38.02	126.27
School Lunch	4.4	6.2	19.75	44.51	64.26
AFDC	5.8	3.0	75.52	21.21	96.73
AFDC, Medicaid, School Lunch, and School Breakfast	1.0	5.3	112.56	14.84	127.40
Any combination including Unemployment Compensation	.8	4.1	68.24	31.96	132.16
Any Combination including Veterans' Benefit	3.4	3.3	96.40	19.96	116.36
All Food Stamp Households (including other benefit categories)	100.0	3.2	74.30	39.41	113.71

Source: U.S. Congress, Joint Economic Committee (1974b, pp. 30–35).

[a]Public transfer income, including cash income equivalents of in-kind benefits derived by computing national average federal cost per recipient, excluding any state or local administrative expenses. Values of medicaid and medicare benefits were computed as follows: If the respondent reported that household members had received subsidized health care in November 1973, and if the respondent could estimate the cost of that care, his or her estimate was used. If no care had been received in that month but the respondent reported coverage under medicaid or medicare, or if care was received but its cost could not be estimated, a national average figures was used.

[b]Although many other benefit combinations were observed (e.g., Food Stamps and Medicaid), each of these many combinations, by themselves, account for only a trivial proportion of the entire food stamp caseload.

TABLE B.4

A Comparison of Annualized Average Incomes of Multiple-Benefit Food Stamp Households with the Farm and Nonfarm Poverty Guidelines for 1973

Benefit in combination with food stamps	Average household income, annualized[a]	1973 Nonfarm poverty lines[b]	1973 Farm poverty line	Ratio of average household income to the nonfarm poverty line
No other program	2584	3250	2763	.80
Social Security	2393	2620	2227	.91
Social Security and Medicare	2655	2550	2168	1.04
General Assistance	3030	2200	1870	1.33
School Lunch	4781	6840	4966	.69
AFDC	3843	3600	3060	1.07
AFDC, Medicaid, School Lunch and School Breakfast	8103	5210	4429	1.55
Any combination including Unemployment Compensation	6502	4370	3715	1.49
Any combination including Veterans' Benefits	4608	3810	3239	1.21

Source: U.S. Congress, Joint Economic Committee (1974b, p. 39).

[a] Equal's average monthly total income per person from Table B.3, multiplied by 12, times the average household size.

[b] Farm and nonfarm poverty lines were computed from the Community Services Administration Poverty Guidelines, for each benefit combination's average household size.

TABLE B.5

Monthly Wage and Salary Incomes Transfer Incomes, and Combined Incomes per Person for May 1973 Households Eligible[a] for Food Stamps, by Participant – Nonparticipant Status in Selected Benefit Categories

Multiple benefit category	Average number of persons per household		Average monthly transfer income per person		Average monthly wage and salary income per person		Average combined income per person[b]	
	Nonparticipants	Participants	Nonparticipants	Participants	Nonparticipants	Participants	Nonparticipants	Participants
Social Security	1.59	1.76	$94.64	$93.04	$4.89	$7.15	$99.53	$100.19
OAA, APID, or AB	1.10	1.11	113.73	134.51	.61	.00	113.89	134.51
AFDC or AFDC-UP	4.18	4.18	41.36	59.05	17.80	6.29	59.16	65.34
General Assistance	1.96	1.75	63.56	98.42	14.44	5.52	78.00	103.94
No cash transfers	4.22	5.26	.00	12.29	62.89	50.28	62.89	62.57
All categories[c]	2.83	3.08	29.81	58.21	43.64	17.29	73.45	75.50

Source: U.S. Bureau of the Census (1973).

[a]Household gross income was less than 125% of the poverty line.

[b]Combined income is the sum of transfer income (including bonus food stamps, if any) and wage and salary income. Thus it excludes unearned income or in-kind income except food stamps.

[c]Refers to all categories specified in this table, not to all food stamp households.

TABLE B.6

Estimated Annual Increments in Average Household Income from Food Stamp Participation, for Selected Benefit Categories

Multiple benefit category	Annualized average income		Increment attributed to bonus food stamps
	Nonparticipants	Participants[a]	
Social Security	$1899	$1911	$12
OAA, APTD, or AB	1503	1775	272
Social Security and OAA, APTD, or AB	1824	2147	323
AFDC or AFDC-UP	2967	3277	310
General Assistance	1834	2445	611
No cash transfers	3185	3168	−17
Total	*2494*	*2564*	70

Source: Table B.5.

[a]Computed by standardizing for the average household size of nonparticipants in each category. For example, the average household size of participants in the Social Security category was 1.76. To get the standardized participant income, multiply the average annual participant income per person by the average household size (1.59) for nonparticipants.

References

Abdel-Ghany, M. (1974) Influences of U.S. urban household characteristics on nutritive intakes and quality of food consumption. Unpublished doctoral dissertation, University of Missouri, Columbia.

Bawden, D. L. (1970) Income maintenance and the rural poor: An experimental approach. *American Journal of Agriculture Economics, 52,* 438–441.

Bickel, G., and MacDonald, M. (1975) Participation rates in the food stamp program: Estimated levels for 1974, by state. *Legal Action Support Project Papers on Poverty and Law.* Washington, D.C.: Bureau of Social Science Research, Inc.

Blechman, B. M., Rivlin, A., and Schultze, C. (1975) *Setting national priorities.* Washington, D.C.: The Brookings Institution.

Bryant, W. K. (1973) Food, food stamps, and the poor. Department of Consumer Economics and Public Policy, New York State College of Human Ecology, Cornell University, Ithaca, New York. Mimeo.

Burke, V. J., and Burke, V. (1974) *Nixon's good deed: Welfare reform.* New York: Columbia University Press.

Citizens Board of Inquiry into Hunger and Malnutrition in the United States. (1968) *Hunger U.S.A.* New York: New Community Press.

Clarkson, K. W. (1975) Food stamps and nutrition. Washington, D.C.: American Enterprise Institute for Public Policy Research.

Clarkson, K. W. (1976) Welfare benefits of the food stamp program. *Southern Economic Journal, 43,* 869.

Coder, J. F. (1975) *Characteristics of households purchasing food stamps in 1974.* Washington, D.C.: U.S. Bureau of the Census.

Coe, R. D. (1977) *Participation in the food stamp program among the poverty population.* Survey Research Center, Institute for Social Research, University of Michigan.

Community Services Administration (1975) *Poverty guidelines for the continental United States.* Washington, D.C.: U.S. Government Printing Office.

Congressional Budget Office (1976) Budget options for the federal food stamp program: Income or food supplementation? Draft, September.

Coppock, J. D. (1947) The food stamp plan. *Transactions of the American Philosophical Society, 37,* 131–200.

Edgar, G. (1973) Dependency: Court rulings on legislative efforts to limit eligibility for government benefits. *Institute for Research on Poverty, Notes and Comments.* Madison, Wisconsin: Institute for Research on Poverty.

Evans, R., Jr., Friedman, B. L., and Hausman, L. J. (1976) The impact of work tests on the employment behavior of welfare recipients. Unpublished manuscript. Waltham, Massachusetts: Brandeis University.

Federal Register (1975) Amendments to the food stamp act of 1964, Volume 40, Nos. 6 and 7. Washington, D.C.: National Archives.

Feltner, R. L. (1975) Statement before the Senate Committee on Agriculture and Forestry. U.S. Department of Agriculture, Office of the Assistant Secretary of Agriculture. Washington, D.C.

Food Research and Action Center (1975) *Outreach regulations.* Washington D.C., 2011 I Street, N.W. 20006.

Food Research and Action Center (1976) *Guide to the food stamp program.* Washington, D.C., 2011 I Street, N.W. 20006.

Forscht, R. D. and Platt, R. (1976) *Income distribution of food stamp households.* Economic Analysis and Program Evaluation Staff. USDA Food and Nutrition Service. Program Evaluation Report (PER) -1, September. Washington, D.C.: U.S. Government Printing Office.

Galatin, M. (1973) A comparison of the benefits of the food stamp program, free food stamps, and equivalent cash payments. *Public Policy,* Spring, 291–302.

Hausman, L. J. (1975) Cumulative tax rates in alternative income maintenance systems. In *Integrating income maintenance programs,* ed. I. Lurie, pp. 39–78. New York: Academic Press.

Hines, F. K. (1972) *Relationship between program participation and level of economic activity.* U.S. Department of Agriculture, Economic Research Service. Washington, D.C.: U.S. Government Printing Office.

Hoagland, W. (1976) Federal aid for food assistance. Unpublished manuscript, Congressional Budget Office, February, p. 10.

Holmer, M. (1976) Reasons for the growth of the food stamp program. Paper presented at the Western Economics Association Conference, San Francisco, p. 28.

Hymans, S. and Shapiro, H. (1974) The allocation of household income to food consumption. In *Five thousand American families: Patterns of economic progress,* Vol. II, ed. J. N. Morgan, pp. 253–378. Ann Arbor, Michigan: Survey Research Center.

Lane, S. (1975) Food aid program effects on food expenditures and levels of nutritional achievement of low-income households. Unpublished manuscript, University of California, Department of Agricultural Economics, Davis.

Melichar, E. (1966) Least-squares analysis of economic survey data. In *1965 Proceedings of* the Business and Economics Statistics Section, American Statistical Association, pp. 373–385. Washington, D.C.

MacDonald, M. (1975a) Adjustment of the poverty measure based on estimates of the food stamp subsidy. Unpublished paper on contract from Office of the Assistant Secretary for Education, U.S. Department of Health, Education, and Welfare.

MacDonald, M. (1975b) *Food stamp program participation in Wisconsin. Institute for Research on Poverty, Notes and Comments.* Madison, Wisconsin: Institute for Research on Poverty.

Madden, P. J. and Yoder, M. D. (1972) *Program evaluation: Food stamps and commodity distribution in rural areas of central Pennsylvania.* Pennsylvania State University Agricultural Experiment Station Bulletin 780, University Park, Pennsylvania.

Mittelhammer, R. and West, D. A. (1974) Food stamp participation among low-income households: Theoretical considerations of the impact on the demand for food. Unpublished manuscript, Washington State University, Pullman.

Morgan, J. N. et al. (1972) *A panel study of income dynamics: study design, procedures, available data.* Ann Arbor, Michigan: University of Michigan Survey Research Center.

Morrill, W. A. (1979) Introduction to the symposium articles. *Journal of Human Resources, 9,* 157.

Nathan, R. P. (1975) The role of the food stamp program. Testimony before the Senate Select Committee on Nutrition and Human Needs. In *Food stamps: the statement of Hon. William E. Simon, Secretary of Treasury,* p. 109. Washington: U.S. Government Printing Office.

National Academy of Sciences—National Research Council. (1974) *Recommended dietary allowances,* 8th ed. Washington, D.C.: National Academy of Sciences.

Nicholson, W. (1973) Expenditure patterns in the graduated work incentive experiment. In *The final report of the New Jersey graduated work incentives experiment,* p. 12. Madison, Wisconsin: Institute for Research on Poverty.

O'Connor, J. F., Madden, J. P., and Prindle, A. M. (1975) The negative income tax as a means of improving nutritional levels among low-income families. Paper prepared for the U.S. Department of Health, Education, and Welfare. Pennsylvania State University, University Park.

Panel Study of Income Dynamics (1975) Data tape for Wave VIII. Ann Arbor: University of Michigan Survey Research Center.

Peskin, J. (1975) The shelter deduction in the food stamp program. Office of Income Security Policy Technical Analysis Paper No. 6, U.S. Department of Health, Education and Welfare. Washington, D.C.: U.S. Government Printing Office.

Peskin, J. (1976) In-kind income and the measurement of poverty. Office of Income Security Policy, U.S. Department of Health, Education, and Welfare. Washington, D.C.: U.S. Government Printing Office.

Primus, W. (1977) A note of caseload turnover within the food stamp program. Preliminary draft, Georgetown University, Washington, D.C.

Rungeling, B. and Smith, L. H. (1975) Factors affecting food stamp nonparticipation in the rural South. *Center for Manpower Studies Paper,* University of Mississippi.

Schlossberg, K. (1975) Funny money is serious. *New York Times Magazine,* September 28, p. 12.

Seagrave, C. (1975) Food stamps and the 1975 recession. Prepared for the Office of Income Security Policy and Analysis, U.S. Department of Health, Education, and Welfare. Washington, D.C.

Sexauer, B., Blank, R., and Kinnucan, H. (1976) Participation in Minnesota's food stamp program. *Minnesota Agricultural Economist,* No. 576. St. Paul: Agricultural Extension Service, University of Minnesota.

Sexauer, B. (1977) In defense of the food stamp program. *University of Minnesota Department of Agricultural and Applied Economics Staff Paper P77-4.* St. Paul: University of Minnesota.

Smeeding, T. (1975) Measuring the economic welfare of low-income households, and the antipoverty effectiveness of cash and noncash-transfer programs. Unpublished doctoral dissertation, University of Wisconsin, Madison.

Smeeding, T. (1977) Food stamp alternatives and poverty. Unpublished manuscript, Department of Economics, University of Utah.

Smolensky, E., Stiefel, L., Schmundt, M., and Plotnick, R. (1974) *Adding in-kind transfers to the personal income and outlay account: implications for the size distribution of income. Institute for Research on Poverty Discussion Paper 199-74.* Madison, Wisconsin: Institute for Research on Poverty.

Steiner, G. (1971) *The state of welfare.* Washington, D.C.: Brookings Institution.

Symposium on the New Jersey Experiment. (1974) *Journal of Human Resources, 9,* 156–158.

Thurow, L. C. (1974) Cash versus in-kind transfers. *American Economic Review, 64,* 190–195.

U.S. Bureau of the Census (1973) *Current population survey.* June. Washington, D.C.: U.S. Government Printing Office.

U.S. Bureau of the Census (1976a) Characteristics of households purchasing food stamps. *Current Population Reports Special Studies, Series P-23,* No. 61, Table 1. Washington, D.C.: U.S. Government Printing Office.

U.S. Bureau of the Census (1976b) Characteristics of the population below the poverty level: 1974. *Current Population Reports, Consumer Income Series P-6,* No. 102, Tables 3 and 17. Washington, D.C.: U.S. Government Printing Office.

U.S. Congress, Joint Economic Committee, Subcommittee on Fiscal Policy (1974a) Public welfare and work incentives: theory and practice. *Studies in public welfare,* No. 14. Washington, D.C.: U.S. Government Printing Office.

U.S. Congress, Joint Economic Committee, Subcommittee on Fiscal Policy (1974b) National survey of food stamp and food distribution recipients. *Studies in Public welfare,* No. 17. Washington, D.C.: U.S. Government Printing Office.

U.S. Congress, Joint Economic Committee, Subcommittee on Fiscal Policy (1975) Handbook of public income transfer programs: 1975. *Studies in public welfare,* No. 20. Washington, D.C.: U.S. Government Printing Office.

U.S. Department of Agriculture, Consumer and Marketing Service (1962) *The food stamp program, an initial evaluation of pilot projects.* Washington, D.C.: U.S. Government Printing Office.

U.S. Department of Agriculture (1973) News release, "Food stamp program expanded."

U.S. Department of Agriculture, Food and Nutrition Service (1973) Summary of work registration acivity for July 1972 through June 1973. Washington, D.C.

U.S. Department of Agriculture, Food and Nutrition Service (1974) Staff Program Report. Washington, D.C.

U.S. Department of Agriculture, Food and Nutrition Service (1975) Table of monthly coupon allotments and purchase requirements for January-June 1975. Washington, D.C.

U.S. Department of Health, Education and Welfare (1973) Public assistance programs: standards for basic needs. Washington, D.C.

U.S. Department of Health, Education, and Welfare, National Center for Health Statistics (1974) *Preliminary findings of the first health and nutrition examination survey, United States 1971–1972: Dietary intake and biochemical findings.* Washington, D.C.: U.S. Government Printing Office.

U.S. House of Representatives, Agriculture Committee Staff (1976) *Costs and comparative analysis of food stamp alternatives.* Staff report, May 18. Washington, D.C.: U.S. Government Printing Office.

U.S. House of Representatives (1976) *Food Stamp Act of 1976: Report on H.R. 13613, 94th Cong., 2nd Sess.,* Report No. 94-1460. Washington, D.C.: U.S. Government Printing Office.

U.S. Senate, Committee on Agriculture and Forestry (1964) *The food stamp program and commodity distribution.* 88th Cong. 2nd Sess. Washington, D.C.: U.S. Government Printing Office.

U.S. Senate, Committee on Agriculture and Forestry (1975) *Food stamp act of 1964 and proposed reform legislation.* 94th Cong. 2nd Sess. Washington, D.C.: U.S. Government Printing Office.

U.S. Senate, Committee on Agriculture and Forestry (1976) *National food stamp reform act of 1976.* 94th Cong. 2nd Sess. Washington, D.C.: U.S. Government Printing Office.

U.S. Senate, Select Committee on Nutrition and Human Needs (1969) Poverty, malnutrition and federal food assistance programs, a statistical summary. 91st Cong. 1st Sess. Washington, D.C.: U.S. Government Printing Office.

U.S. Senate, Select Committee on Nutrition and Human Needs (1974) Panel on Nutrition and Special Groups. *National Nutrition Policy Study Report and Recommendations, VIII.* Washington, D.C.: U.S. Government Printing Office.

U.S. Senate, Select Committee on Nutrition and Human Needs (1976) *Food stamp program profile: Part I.* Washington, D.C.: U.S. Government Printing Office.

Weisbrod, B. (1970) *On the stigma effect and demand for welfare programs: a theoretical note. Institute for Research on Poverty Discussion Paper 82-70.* Madison, Wisconsin: Institute for Research on Poverty.

A
B 7
C 8
D 9
E 0
F 1
G 2
H 3
I 4
J 5